Song of the
Streams

Song of the
Streams

———

MICHELLE
WERRETT

Photography by
ROBIN BAKER

THE
MEDLAR PRESS
ELLESMERE

Published by The Medlar Press Limited,
The Grange, Ellesmere, Shropshire SY12 9DE
www.medlarpress.com

ISBN 978-1-915694-07-2

Text © Michelle Werrett 2023

Design © The Medlar Press 2023

Photographs © Robin Baker 2023

Designed and typeset in 12 on 14 point Garamond Roman.
Produced in England by The Medlar Press Limited, Ellesmere, England.

Contents

ILLUSTRATIONS

Inspiration

CHAPTER 1

Beginnings

———

Cloud hangs low over the upturned face of the earth where hills arch up to meet it. The moors are often lost for days at a time in the soft embrace of fog, the peaty soils and spongy mosses wet and swollen by rain. From this coupling of earth and sky the streams of Exmoor are born. Oozing through rushes, seeping through sedge grass, the slow drainings become a trickle soon joined by others, quickly gaining strength and speed. Their voices, answering the wind of the hills, are the endless songs of the valleys.

Between Chapman Barrows in the west and Dunkery Beacon to the east, the high spine of the moor divides streams running south towards Devon from those taking the short route north to the sea. In places this spine is very narrow – the deep bogs of The Chains drain northwards to become the West Lyn and south into Pinkworthy Pond, the beginning of the River Barle. Longstone Barrow marks the point between water running north into the Barbrook and south to the River Bray. A spur of Hoaroak Water, another tributary of the Lyn, begins only yards from Exe Head, the rising of the great river that will travel right across Devon to the English Channel.

This moorland spine is marked by a chain of barrows strung across the land by our Bronze Age ancestors. The names, faces, voices and even language of those ancient people have long been erased from a land that must have altered beyond their recognition, only the streams continue in their same wild ways. The barrows were built for housing the dead yet they also honour this place of births and arisings from where the infant streams set forth, chattering and chuckling as they go, sinuous as otter, sparkling as dipper song, etching the goyles, cutting the combes, carving the shape of the land in their journeys from cloud to sea.

* * *

The foothills of Exmoor were a tantalising place to grow up. My home nestled among meadows, woodlands and hedges, within sound of heron-kraak, curlew-cry and river-murmur but, like an adventure waiting to happen, the moors lay just beyond my reach. In my longing to explore that wild and beautiful land where it seemed tales of the old days still played on I read everything I could find about Exmoor, rapaciously hunting out books from my mother's shelves and from the local library.

One such book was Claude Wade's *Exmoor Streams – Notes and Jottings with Practical Hints for Anglers*, published in 1903 with reminiscences from the previous forty years or so, and I was captivated by the glimpse of familiar places illuminated in the light of a different century. Wade wrote engagingly of rivers, landscape, inns and some of the characters he encountered along the lanes in much the way he might have fondly addressed a grandchild with tales of his youth. When growing independence enabled me to walk or ride over the moors without restraint I was delighted to find the rivers and streams apparently little altered from his description.

Many years later, as an enthusiastic but not very experienced fly fisherman, I opened his pages again. This time I was seeking advice about fishing but found so much more. What especially struck me were his accounts of fish catches that seem fantastic by modern standards; where I should have been content with three or four trout in an afternoon, Wade regularly caught several dozen leaving me in awe of the abundance he must have encountered. Learning to fish brought a new and more intimate perspective to my view of Exmoor streams and aroused deep concern for their wellbeing.

And I wondered how it would be to fish where Wade fished, to cast the same flies on the same pools of those babbling moorland streams. So that's what I determined to do. From his writing and advice I might learn something more about fly fishing, I reasoned, and as a relative beginner I had a great deal more to learn. Most of all, I wanted to find out how fishing Exmoor streams might compare with fishing them a century and a half ago, whether those streams have changed and how they might be faring today. In our modern world of intensive agriculture and spreading urbanisation, moorlands and the streams threading through them appear to have a timeless quality which, for a working, food producing landscape, feels close to an undefiled state of grace. Surely here, at least, I might discover a remnant of unspoilt nature, untarnished by the years.

We are all subject to a phenomenon known as 'shifting baseline syndrome', which basically means we have short memories. As the world around us changes we come to accept the new state of things, constantly updating our expectations of what is normal. This can lead us to believe that our rivers and streams have always been the same, lulling us into a complacency that all is well, unless we take the trouble to unearth records of the past. Old fishermen are rich repositories of tales from earlier times when, they tell us, there were more fish and bigger fish in the rivers than there are today; yet even the most venerable of these characters can have no personal experience of rivers over a hundred years ago. Several organisations carry out river monitoring surveys of various kinds but none have data going back more than a few decades to serve as a standard against which today's rivers can be judged. Wade was writing in 1902 of memories stretching back to 1861 and the changes he witnessed over the intervening years. How much more change, for better and worse, there must have been since. Perhaps the most valuable aspect of Wade's work is its unique record of the quality of rivers in those early days and in assertion of its truth he asks, 'May my readers believe me.' I have no reason to doubt him.

The Exmoor coastal village of Lynmouth that Claude Wade discovered was on the cusp of change from obscure fishing village to popular holiday resort. During the seventeenth and eighteenth centuries the young of wealthy families completed their classical education by touring around Europe to learn about culture, language and art in a tradition known as The Grand Tour; but when the Napoleonic Wars brought this improving travel to a halt alternative destinations were sought within our own shores. At around the same time, the Industrial Revolution dragged a generation of rural people into towns and cities to work in 'dark satanic mills', creating a nostalgia for the countryside of their youth, yet also sufficient wealth to enable many of them to take holidays.

One reaction to the suffocating new urbanisation was Romanticism, a movement idealising nature and glorifying the past in arts, music and literature. Poets including Southey, Coleridge and Wordsworth visited and wrote about Exmoor, enrapturing its beauty, romanticising its wildness and entrancing those in search of fresh intellectual stimulus or an escape from smoke blackened, smog choked cities. When Blackmoor's novel *Lorna Doone* was published in 1869 the romantic perception of Exmoor as an idyllic resort was firmly established.

That tourists were slow to reach Exmoor, and its charm when they did, was largely due to its inaccessibility; yet throughout the nineteenth century demand grew and provision of transport and accommodation was quick to service it. From 1830 steamships stopped at Lynmouth where, if the sea was not too rough, passengers could be ferried ashore by rowing boat. Soon, hotels and guest houses were built and four-horse stagecoaches ran with increasing frequency on rapidly improving roads. Railways reached Dulverton and Barnstaple, on the periphery of the moor, in 1873 and Minehead the following year. Almost at once, coaches were co-ordinated with train times so that it became possible to travel from London to Exmoor in just one day.

As travel became available to newly-monied middle classes desperate for respite from the grim urban source of their wealth, its primary purpose changed – the focus on education was replaced by a need for relaxation and pleasure. Hotels promoted pastimes such as sea-bathing, walking, hunting and fishing and the availability of hotel water for guests to fish became a major attraction ranking alongside a stable of fit mannerly horses and soon to be joined by the marvels of electric light and hot and cold running water. The Exmoor fishing holiday was born.

Fishing rights became a desirable amenity for hotels and were often the subject of much negotiation and disagreement. The Carnarvon Arms Hotel near Dulverton was originally built to service a livestock market but enlarged to accommodate grow-ing numbers of anglers and, in 1900, it was considered that the fishing rights virtually doubled its rental value. William Bevan, proprietor of the Lyndale and Tor Hotels at Lynmouth, regu-larly advertised in *The Fishing Gazette* boasting access to twenty miles of the best trout, salmon and peal fishing. His son, Cecil Bevan, who took over the Lyn Valley Hotel, personally accom-panied guests both on rivers and by boat at sea. Before long, hotels employed experienced fishermen to act as guide and tutor to visiting anglers; Fred Tout and then Bill Thorne both became legends in performing this office for the Carnarvon Arms Hotel.

Claude Wade came to holiday on Exmoor in the midst of all this development. At first, as a twelve year old boy, it seems likely he was brought by his parents, and as both were born into families of army officers in India where his father became a much celebrated Colonel (he was the first man to force the Khyber Pass) they could afford to travel and would have been undaunted by adventuring to remote parts of England, however primitive the transport.

Wade tells us of travelling by horse drawn coach along the main routes and by a hired carriage or trap on smaller ones, and how conveniently the driver can be made to wait while you fish or be sent on to collect you at the end of the day from another point on the river. We are warned to take a good thick coat, even in summer, for the evening drive home over high moorland roads in an open trap.

With growing numbers of holidaymakers, fish such as salmon, peal, or sea trout, and even little brown trout became increasingly valuable commodities for busy hotel kitchens and unscrupulous harvesting by all manner of unfair and foul means depleted their numbers, while the River Lyn became notorious for rampant poaching and bad practice, deterring honest fishermen from visiting. Wade witnessed realisation amongst the people of Lynton and Lynmouth that considerably more money could be made from fishing tourists than through poaching and saw the growth of a general consensus and support to protect the River Lyn as an asset. Fishing tourism was the saving of the river and its fish.

The Victorian Exmoor Wade knew was a bustling, fast-changing place. People with strange accents, different clothes and, no doubt, baffling ideas came to the area for both work and leisure. Exmoor was gaining a more worldly complexion but perhaps losing a vernacular innocence as each visitor un-wittingly eroded a little of the charm they had come to find.

Local characters, including landowners such as Nicholas Snow and Sir Frederick Knight, appear in Wade's book along-side the nice old lady from Cloud Farm who would yarn to you for hours, Mr Kingdon, the postmaster and blacksmith from Simonsbath who would tell you all about the fishing and could also pull out teeth if you happened to be troubled that way, and the poor old tailor from Lynton with a keen pointed nose, dressed in old shiny black clothes, carrying his seedy looking rod and basket and a bag of worms.

What tales they could have told and how I wish I could have met them. But if the Victorian characters and carriages have gone the rivers have not. Much has changed on Exmoor over the intervening years but the streams still run free through farmland, woods and moors and trout still lie in the dappled pools, yet surely not in the numbers they did to enable Wade to catch 167 in one eight hour day or to justify his tale of Parson Gould catching over 300 and having to requisition carts to bring the spoil home.

Wade's tales of astonishing fish abundance are corroborated by other writers who recorded their own long-ago experiences of Exmoor waters. Claude Luttrell backs up Wade's account of Exmoor fishing and adds the interesting perspective of the River Avill at Dunster where, he tells us, brown trout and sea trout were once unbelievably large and numerous. Their stories are supported by Reverend William Thornton, who also fished the Avill and the Horner as well as other Exmoor streams during the mid nineteenth century. Even in those days, Thornton remarks that trout seemed to be thicker in the streams years before and that sport generally was not so good as in the days of his youth whilst, worryingly, both Wade and Luttrell tell us that numbers of salmon and trout were declining. The ugly question of whether those immodest catches of the nineteenth century might have left a scarcity of fish in today's streams demanded investigation.

Two more fishing writers, Arthur Applin and Negley Farson, both stayed at the Carnarvon Arms Hotel and wrote of pulling impressive fish from its waters on the rivers Exe and Barle. From another local nucleus of sporting hospitality, the Tarr Steps Hotel, we can learn a lot about the River Barle through memories collected in the visitors' fishing record book. It is inestimably sad that these hotels have closed their doors and this loss, with its significant effect on the local community, is not unrelated to the fortunes of fish. When salmon were plentiful, holidays fishing on hotel waters were aspired to, dreamed of and saved for by fishermen from far and wide. Trout and salmon were proudly displayed on platters in hotel lobbies and details entered in record books to encourage recent arrivals with news of the previous week's sport. Guests' record cards would often be annotated with the instruction, 'Telephone when the salmon are running.'

All these memories provide priceless records of the state of rivers and their fish in faraway days, and the words of those long gone fishermen, like back eddies beside the relentless current, remember a golden age of plenty. Wade, Luttrell, Thornton and the rest regularly caught numbers of fish which, a century or more later, seem unbelievable when today half a dozen trout might be considered respectable and salmon are rarely encountered. The pristine appearance of upland streams disguise troubled hearts but it is encouraging to meet many people dedicated to their restoration and to achieving a better future for our land. Rivers flow only onwards, and though we may be able to travel throughout the world we cannot return to those sepia-tinted summers of the past. Yet on Exmoor today the waters still run on in their wild ways, there are even now a few interesting characters about and trout can still, sometimes, be seduced by a well considered fly.

The River Barle

CHAPTER 2

Autumn Amber

———

On an amber day of honey-rich autumn sunshine I bumped along a moorland track to park on the rocky eminence above Sherdon Hutch, where Sherdon Water meets the River Barle. From this point there is a good view of the valley with the river twisting its way between hills where green bracken was dappled with tan, rushes and moor grass had ripened to the colour of caramel and spires of bog asphodel glowed a deep vibrant copper. In anticipation I pulled on waders as fast as I could, put up a six foot rod and stuffed my pockets with various tins of flies and, of course, chocolate. A wading stick I considered unnecessary as in low water I find it more hindrance than help. Wade says of the Barle, 'The lower water up from Sherdon Hutch I liked best, numbers were less but size better, and most of the water perfect for the fly.' I like it too and it is still perfect for the fly.

Wade explains that Sir Frederick Knight, the Victorian owner of Exmoor Forest, used formerly to give tickets to fish this water but that it had been made available to visitors staying at the Exmoor Forest Hotel in Simonsbath and he recommends communicating with the landlord and having breakfast at the hotel, your trap being made to wait. Day tickets to fish can still be bought from the hotel, as can breakfast or coffee to set you off to a good start, but most people nowadays use motor vehicles and drive themselves.

Wade recommends wearing waders for this stretch of river where, he says, wading is really useful whilst on all the other streams in his book it is 'almost a sin to do it at all and is absolutely unnecessary'. I personally find wading a great help on almost all waters and don't think I could fish many places without doing so but was pleased to have Wade's confirmation that, on this river at least, wading was the correct procedure.

I scrambled down a goyle through tall, tangling bracken and stumbled through tussocky grasses and sedges at the bottom to reach the river. As I fished up towards the pool at Sherdon Hutch I had half an eye open for tourists that often swarm there to picnic and swim. There were not many but one was particularly troublesome. A man in a red T-shirt threw sticks across the river for his terrier who swam back and forth enthusiastically and as I waded up the river trying to get past him he walked along the bank keeping ahead of me. I'm sure it wasn't deliberate, he probably wasn't very bright, but it was vexing nonetheless. At the junction pool I climbed out onto the far bank of the Barle and, with the Sherdon Water between us, was able to leave him behind. And to leave everyone and everything else as I wandered blissfully into heaven.

As I picked my way up the river I worked my way into the water, into the ripples and eddies of the laughing current that washed everything else away. The river was glass clear, just faintly tinged with peaty amber, the colour of a whisky and soda and the pebbly bed was clean. After half an hour, had I encountered anyone else playing with a dog in the river I should have smiled benignly and might have thrown a stick, but it didn't happen again. I didn't see another soul all day.

After fishing the River Exe near home it was a refreshing change to fish between banks clear of trees. There must be only three withies on the whole beat and I lost flies in every one of them. (I was, as I say, a very inexperienced fisherman.) The first stretch of river runs between moorland on either side, then above Sherdon Hutch there is rough, marshy ground sheltered by steep, brackeny cleaves. A little further along, on the northern flank of the valley, Pickedstones Plantation had been clear felled of its once oppressively dark conifers and the site colonised by rough herbs and grasses leaving a light open feeling of relief.

To the south, the slopes of Ferny Ball bordered by beech hedges rose to the sky bringing me scraps of remembered conversations with my dear friend, Hope, who once lived there. She was a tiny, wild figure scented with woodsmoke, her smile etched deeply into the wrinkles of her face. I remembered her telling me about a large salmon she once found on the bank here. It had been killed by an otter who had taken little of the flesh leaving most of it, quite fresh, for her supper.

Wade writes of the 'splendid pools and bends in the river just here' and so they are. I cast a simple Deer Hair Sedge fly into pools and pockets, searching the seams of the stream, and caught a small trout, silvery body flashing as he flipped in the sunlight. When I released him he swam off with a spurt of wriggling speed. The little ones have so much energy, they always make me smile and sometimes laugh out loud at their quick infectious joy.

Wade advises that 'a south wind is the best for casting on this reach, and a north-west wind the most difficult'. I found myself with a brisk easterly and made several mistakes before I could gauge how much further into the gusty wind I should aim my cast to put the fly in the right spot.

A little further along there was a bend with a series of riffles and rocks at the reunion of two streams below a small island. This looked a likely place, I thought, and when I cast into it was rewarded with the cheerful 'sploop' of a rising fish but he did not take the fly. It was a good fish though and I determined to try for him again. I sat on the bank, ate some chocolate and changed my fly for a small Adams tied with a mole fur body and a fine tail. Ravens quocked behind me, a buzzard ki-aowed overhead and a little sandpiper flew upstream on sharply tapered wings.

When I cast into the pool again I had him. A beautiful plump Barle trout, the light gold of moor grass speckled with shades of heather stem and bracken, each spot haloed in soft light – the colours of the land around me.

To catch such a splendid fish was a delight but Wade would probably have been unimpressed. His trout were not large, he tells us that his best basket in weight and condition of fish was 'sixty-six weighing twelve pounds', so averaging around three ounces, I think. He did catch a lot though, and wrote that he many times had between eighty and a hundred and once a hundred and three in a day. Such numbers were unimaginable to me but the smile they put on Wade's face cannot have been brighter than the smile my one beautiful fish brought to mine. I fished on along the bright stream between banks fringed with bracken and moor grass and the only thing that did not look quite natural were the curved blades of montbretia. It is sad to see so much of this foreign invader, which has become firmly established, spreading alarmingly along the banks of the Barle. Running water is particularly efficient at carrying seeds or root fragments so that plants quickly colonise downstream, making riverbanks worryingly vulnerable to invasive species like this. I can only just remember a time when there was very little of it here. At least, I think I can. All I really remember, perhaps around the early 1990s, is suddenly noticing such a lot of this new plant and wondering what it was. My attention was only drawn by its magnitude.

Many non-native species are out of balance with the native ones and can entirely obliterate them from an area. Not all non-natives are so aggressive – the Molland lily, for example, a native of the Pyrenees Mountains, grows wild in hedges on the southern side of Exmoor where it appears to live quite equitably amongst its neighbours, but montbretia does not. In their natural state these riverbanks would likely have primroses, violets and celandines in spring; tormentil, eyebright, louse-wort, bedstraws and bird's-foot-trefoil in summer. But in some stretches all of these wildflowers have been replaced by this one plant which does not flower before late summer, until then simply smothering the banks with its long leaves so that all invertebrates searching for pollen and nectar must go elsewhere. This banishing of insects from the riverbank surely has an impact on the insectivorous lives of the stream; dippers, wagtails and trout must all notice a depletion in their food supply and fewer of them may survive as a result. In summer, water-fallen terrestrial creatures can form between fifty and ninety percent of trout diet. Human engineered change, whether deliberate or accidental, often leads to unintended and ill-considered consequences.

I once asked Dennis about montbretia. He used to farm here and knew the land better than anyone so I thought would be sure to know when it arrived but he said he had never noticed. Often those closest to a problem notice it least as, when we see a place daily, gradual change can be too easy to miss.

The Barle is a river I have known all my life. I paddled in it as a child catching bullheads or mollyheads as we called them, lifting the broad stones they hid under and scooping them up in my hands. I have ridden its banks and forded its crossings on iron-shod legs far swifter and more foot-sure than my own, from its birth at Pinkworthy Pond on Exmoor Forest to The Meeting of The Waters where it finally joins the River Exe. So the Barle is a river I already feel at home with and fishing it draws us closer, brings our relationship a deeper meaning, a more defined purpose, so that I am elevated from frequent visitor to family member. The deepest joy of fishing is the intimacy it brings with the river but the magic really starts earlier than that. It really starts with tying flies.

On my daily wanderings I like to collect bits and pieces I can use to tie into fishing flies; sheep's wool from brambles, corrugated deer hair from barbed wire, a feather dropped by a jay, joyfully barred with black and speedwell blue – treasures gleaned from the land. Jack, a neighbouring farmer, traps moles in fields he plans to mow because if soil from their mounds gets into silage it can cause a fatal disease called listeria in animals who eat it. He brings me their soft, compact carcasses from which I cut small squares of sumptuous black velvet and cure them with salt.

Occasionally I accompany friends for a day's shooting or ferreting when it is good to take home a brace of pheasants or rabbits for supper and, of course, I save the feathers or skins. There is a satisfying circularity about using these stunningly beautiful materials harvested from the winter woods and fields to create flies I will use to catch trout in a summer stream. In this way I feel a connection to more than the river and a relationship with more than the fish. A deep network of kinship and affinity is braided through the whole landscape linking deer and woodland, rabbits and river, pheasants and fish, and I feel a heady awareness of being inextricably bound into the interconnected web of all life.

There came a stretch where streaks of dark weed streamed in the current under the right bank and from this weed I enticed several more trout to rise to my fly and though they were very small yet it was, as Wade described, perfect moorland fishing. High on the steep cleave of Horsen Brake to my left, a hind and calf picked their way quietly through bracken while on my right, where the steep ramparts of Cow Castle topped with its Iron Age hillfort reared above me, a raven spoke from the sky. The deep valley, free of all other human presence, was utterly at peace.

The east wind strengthened in the afternoon, so that I found it increasingly difficult to put the fly down on the water without a splash and the fish seemed to lose interest. At length, the sun dropped below the round shoulder of Great Woolcombe dragging the temperature down with it. Unlike Wade, I did not have a carriage with a driver to send on to Simonsbath so had to retrace my steps down the riverbank to my patiently waiting vehicle. Nevertheless, after an amber autumn day spent in companionship with the laughter-bright Barle I was unquestionably, as Wade promised, a happy and contented fisherman.

CHAPTER 3

Breakfast Trout

Scraps of chiffon mist hung over steep wooded hillsides like tatters torn from the paling sky. The sun, were it not obscured in cloud, would have been rising. Tarr Steps is a medieval clapper bridge, a rugged heaping together of boulders and massive stone slabs, spanning the River Barle. It is an understandably popular spot for tourists, and would be crowded on an August day, but by fishing so early in the morning I hoped to have the river to myself. So far there was no one to be seen.

In the cool, drizzly conditions there were few insects about so I first tried a small green nymph – one that had been most successful lower down the river last week. I scrambled along the rocky bank, getting into the river here and there, casting into pots and pools and the hurrying bubble line, working my way upstream. Two wagtails skipped along the opposite bank, leapfrogging each other from stone to stone.

This stretch of fishing was once the preserve of the Tarr Steps Hotel; a former Georgian rectory with stables, kennels, rough shooting, three miles of fishing and refreshingly free of television, it was a delightfully comfortable, intimate country-house hotel in the traditional style seldom surviving modern times. Both this one and the Carnarvon Arms sadly closed their doors in 2001, that darkly tragic year when foot and mouth disease devastated the countryside.

The fish showed no interest in my nymph so I tried a wet fly, a Greenwell's Glory, and cast upstream, retrieving line fast to keep pace with the speed of the river, but had no success. Fishing upstream with nymphs or wet flies is tricky when takes can be very subtle and easy to miss in a turbulent current.

The depth under the right bank was increasing and water threatened to overtop my thigh waders so I climbed up the bank between beech and oak trees and scralled up over the covert grasping roots, stems, tussocks of grasses and woodrush, wondering briefly whether they would hold my weight on the precipitous slope. They did; and at length I reached a path and walked along briskly for a while, pausing here and there to taste the bright scarlet sharpness of wild raspberries trailing from the hillside.

At home on my desk lay an old ledger I had been reading, borrowed with promises of careful handling and a prompt return. The tatty board covers are dark, of indeterminate colour, but the new navy spine shows with what care and reverence this treasured volume has been rebound. Columns on the lined pages suggest that the book was designed as a ledger set out to receive figures in pounds, shillings and pence, yet to what heights such lowly material soared. In this book, from 1972 to the year 2000, guests of the Tarr Steps Hotel recorded their fishing successes and failures, their delights, frustrations and achievements in brief summaries of fishing holidays on the River Barle. Here, men, women and children recorded catching their first ever fish, their biggest fish, the most fish and so many personal achievements; some were clearly learning and improving whilst others already had considerable skill and experience. What follows is a small selection:

13 fish – 5 taken remainder returned for next year! Touts Beige. First time. About 20 fish 6 taken all on wet ginger quill. – John

Trout 5" – 7" 24 fish, Touts Beige. 5" About 30 fish, 7 taken.

Water very low. Hot. Best around 9¼" long. Grey Duster. About 50 fish, 8 taken Touts Beige and Pheasant Tail. – Bill

Over 40 fish caught but very few over the 8" limit. Mostly on a Greenwell (wet) and some home tied unidentified. Since first fishing here 25 years ago the trout have not improved in size or condition which seems to prove that there is not enough food to support the population. Saw salmon leap four times in Rectory Pool. Lovely bright, windless afternoon; clouds of fly on the water. Walked up from the Steps and caught 16 trout. Kept 5. Fly believed to be a Partridge and Yellow. – Alwyn

Caught one trout 6 inches long. I caught it with a pheasant tail. – Giles (Age 8)

Excellent fishing, great fun. 3 brace trout from Hunting Bridge and Rectory. Some worthy of breakfast. – AC

This is a hard river in such low conditions but there always seems to be a willing fish somewhere. About a dozen fish in all. Small flies – Pheasant Tail seems as good as anything. A river I really do not want to leave. – John Bailey

Had a pleasant couple of weeks and managed to put most of the trout in the Barle in a dangerous position. Managed to catch a few, at least three able to be eaten for breakfast – that's if we could face them at that time of the morning. Liz managed to catch lots of things – trees, rocks, my hat and one cow – too small for breakfast table so threw it back. – Richard and Liz (not Burton)!

Caught my first ever trout! Not very big but made a good breakfast. – Melanie

Biggest trout yet – 7oz. – Dave

A very enjoyable first day of the season. Two little trout for break-fast. – Michael

Lots of lively fish about! If like me you don't like to walk too far, the meadow will always provide sport and it has the advantage that you can see the bar! Two 'breakfast size' browns to take away. Utterly compulsive!! – David

A very pleasant week taking small trout on dry fly – mainly black gnat, beacon beige and tupp's. Three at 8" to 9" kept. On Thursday afternoon fishing a pheasant tail nymph in rock pool, hooked and landed a rainbow trout that weighed in at 1lb 7oz! It was in good condition and gave a good fight for about ten minutes before coming to the net. Very exciting. – Alan

A welcome break from work, managed to land a monster of at least 4" after a struggle with my hangover. A perfect introduction to this absorbing sport. One brown trout (¾lb) taken on a warm spring evening; now I am 'hooked' as well. – Paul

We fished . . . we shot . . . we drank . . . and drank . . . and drank. In between periods of mellow intoxication we found the river and managed to catch 3 trout of 6 or so inches on the dry fly pheasant tail and olive. Keep the place going. Another marvellous week. No salmon! but the Barle trout were magnificent as usual. 35 fish, one stocky (1½lbs) otherwise all wild and returned except one badly hooked 10" trout. 3 fish 11" or over including one of 13½", an incredible specimen of approx 1½lb was seen and risen on 4 occasions. 'Gilbert' has the girth of a rugger ball and tail of a shovel. I will return!! (All trout taken on an assortment of small dry flies.) – James

In thirty years of fishing in many different countries, I have never come across trout as feisty and as lusty as those in the Barle. It is a joy and a privilege to fish for wild brown trout in conditions

as near natural as those to be found in this delightful river.
– Don

The best trout fishing week I've ever had anywhere, just as I like it.
The Beacon Beige did its job wonderfully. Altogether super.
P.S. Please can I come again! – John

Only a real maniac would have fished a dry fly up that run. And
here was a real maniac. Worth the trouble, however, as I caught 2
trees, 1 bush and a 'breakfast size' trout there. Returned many
trout, took 3 'breakfast size' and one 10oz fish on my last day from
the bottom water in a shallow run. All fish on dry fly, size 14 pheas-
ant tail. A very nice week's fishing. – Paul

Approx 30 trout caught, 5 killed. Largest 1lb 2oz and one of ¾lb,
all taken on dry flies. However, 'Gilbert', although seen on five
occasions, still remains in the Barle to haunt me for another win-
ter. He is in magnificent condition and must be 2lb. He is fat as a
pig and superbly proportioned. I would like to take him on a dry
fly but realistically he will probably fall to a tube fly or, as has been
suggested, will be tailed! The legend lives on. – James

First ever fishing experience – wonderful fun! Caught 4 trout and
2 salmon with pheasant tail fly. All success due to the expert teach-
ing of John Sharp. Will definitely carry on learning to fish. N.B. All
fish 2" long! – Susie and Robin

Caught a half pound brown trout on a coachman in the meadow.
Killed it myself! – Eleanor (age 11)

One and a half days fishing on this lovely river. Sixteen small brown
trout caught and returned. Two 11" and 12" taken. Fly used
reverse tied welsh terrier, perfect for fast stickles. Mollie caught her
first 'brownie' all of 4 inches. – Mollie and Barry

Once again good trout fishing. I won't comment on the salmon! 6 breakfast sized trout and a 1lb 2oz brownie taken with the last cast on a Royal Coachman above Hinds Pit. However, the sad news is that Gilbert has not been seen again, although there is uncon- firmed sighting. There can be no doubt though that he's still there, more magnificent than ever, waiting for a balmy evening next year. – James

My first trout on my own just above Rectory Pool – Tom (age 9)

Three fish, 3lb, 6lb & 8lb, all very fresh. Last fish kindly netted by a passing 'Good Samaritan'. – Audre

One salmon 7lb fresh, Rock Pool, 4pm. Caught by that 'passing Samaritan'. – Richard

My first trout on a dry fly. – Kit (age 8)

First day, first hour, first pool and my first salmon on a fly – noth- ing will ever be quite like it again – 4lb 2oz! Garry fly. Above Hunting Bridge 8am, overcast. – Joanne

My trout was 8½ inches long and I am only 9 years old. – Christopher

The last entry, all rods caught eight fish between them today, very sad day, all fish returned to live another day. We have all had a real fun week, no pressure to catch fish, this total probably doesn't represent the amount of fish we could have caught but everyone is happy to take a fish each home. Many more will be caught over dinner.

Here, so many memories are recorded in handwriting as individual and sometimes as obscure as those long-gone fishermen, several returning year after year, their names often the least discernible of all and sometimes omitted altogether. Yet whoever they were, whatever lives they had briefly stepped away from, all these scribes are largely unconcerned by weather, water conditions, losing flies in trees or getting thoroughly wet; whatever their results, the overriding message behind the records in this book is one of joy.

And my favourite of them all, expressing not only joy but also wonder:

The Barle is a blessed river. The brownies rise far more readily than you might expect – I caught six small ones, one keepable – but not only the trout make for the charm of the valley – we saw king-fishers, grey wagtails, dippers, spotted flycatchers and grey heron. All this and the beechwood too.

Yes, fishing is about so much more than catching fish. The valley, its woods and water and all the wild lives it holds are seen more clearly, experienced more intensely simply because we are fishing. In order to fish successfully we have to notice wind and water, insects hatching, trout feeding, and the imperative to concentrate attention brings the river into such sharp focus that little capacity remains for awareness of troubles in the humancentric world beyond the riverbank. Here, perhaps, was a fisherman who felt as I do – experiencing the elevation of spirit found through an intimate connection with the never-ending river and, amid the fun and exhilaration of fishing, a stillness and sense of reverence which comes close to prayer. The writer goes on to offer the Latin verse, *Omnium fluminum deus beatus, deus Barlensis beatissiums sit*, which translates to something like, 'All river gods are blessed, the god of the Barle is most blessed of all'.

Hind's Pit is a broad, deep pool on a wide sweeping bend where the West Water comes tumbling through the woods and issues into the Barle. Oaks spread solicitous boughs far over the water from the west bank while the east side is open grass and bracken. The current idled through the pool, slow and smooth offering not the faintest ripple to disguise my line and though I waded ever so carefully and degreased the leader, the fine translucent thread between line and fly, my presence must have been obvious to fish in the clear water. The Greenwell's Glory was emphatically ignored.

Entries in the hotel records mention frequent successes with a dry fly called a Tout's Beige or Beacon Beige. This fly was invented by Captain Gilbert Wills, of the Bristol tobacco company family, who served in the Royal North Devon Yeomanry. It was 1917, he was on leave from France and spent that wet summer fishing from his home at Northmoor House, amid deer-threaded oak woodlands of the Barle Valley just a few miles downstream from where I fished that morning. Possibly heavy rain and a river of high, coloured water made fly tying a more attractive option on some days. Anyway, Wills enjoyed great success with the small inconspicuous fly he created, which he called simply a Beige, and gave one to Fred Tout.

Fred Tout sold fishing tackle from his bicycle repair shop in Dulverton which he would leave at any excuse to go fishing, frequently acting as a guide or teacher for visiting fishermen, and regularly found in the tap room of the Carnarvon Arms Hotel. Even in those long-ago days, Fred was concerned about the health of rivers, damage from road run-off and the disappearance of insects. He was described by Negley Farson in *Going Fishing*: 'He stains his own casts and ties his own flies and is so covered with flies stuck into his coat and hat himself that he looks like a veritable cockleburr.' Fred satisfied himself of the effectiveness of the Beige and made copies to sell. Then, after the First War its popularity boomed when *The Field* published a letter from Captain Wills extolling its virtues.

Well, the years rolled on and at the end of World War Two Fred's son, Harry, was demobbed from the Somerset Light

Infantry Motorcycle Platoon and returned home to Dulverton where he helped in his father's shop. One day, looking out between the tall glazing-bars of the shop window, Harry met the eyes of a face peering in at fishing tackle displayed there and he stopped, transfixed. For one brief moment of disbelief he forgot to breathe; then he shouted out in excitement – it was Peter Deane!

Harry dashed out of the shop and with much hand pumping the two men exchanged rapturous greetings. There was so much to catch up on, they had not seen each other since both were in uniform during the early days of the war, it must have been eight years ago. Really, as long as that? Yes, it must be. It was in 1940 at Lydd Camp, Lance Corporal Harry Tout had taught Peter Deane to ride a motorcycle. This was a rather important skill for Deane as he had just been made Commanding Officer in charge of a motorcycle platoon. What fun they had had, that summer on the south east coast before the tides of war swept them apart.

Harry's delight at seeing his old friend was, however, tempered with shock and dismay to find him in a motorised wheelchair. Peter explained that he had contracted polio during a posting to India and now due to his disability, and despite knowing nothing about fishing, had decided to become a professional fly dresser. He had planned to visit the trout hatchery at Exebridge as they advertised natural blue poultry but was disappointed to find it recently closed down, so he wandered into Dulverton and noticed the fishing tackle shop. Their reunion was pure chance.

Harry fetched his father, certain that these two would have much to discuss – and so they did. Old Fred Tout, his hat still bristling with flies, took an instant liking to his son's friend and was most encouraging of his plans for a fly tying business.

"I hopes you do well, boy," he said, lifting down his pipe.

"Good of you to say so, Mr Tout, but I couldn't know less about it," Peter admitted. "I've never been fly fishing in my life."

"Ah, but you can learn. You could make a good go of it – folks have got time to go fishing again now war's over." He searched amongst his fly boxes and picked out three flies.

"Here you are," said Fred. "I'm going to give you these three flies to copy: this one's The Pertwee, this red and white one's called You's Fancy and this one is a Beige. You can sell these, and if you make nothing else you'll never starve." The three little flies offered in tobacco stained fingers were the beginning of a new career for Peter.

As soon as he got home to Hemyock, Peter made some of the rather dull looking Beige flies in preparation for his first fishing lesson the next day. There on the little River Culm, on his first day's fly fishing, his Beige took four brace of trout to eight and a half ounces. Neither of the other two flies Fred Tout had given Peter made much impact but the Beige enjoyed enormous success on many Devon rivers, and later on chalk streams, for both brown trout and sea trout. Peter renamed it the Beacon Beige after Culmstock Beacon, the prominent landmark he looked out on from the window of his fly tying workshop, and went on to sell as many of these as all his other dry fly patterns together. The shop for fishing tackle in Dulverton today is Lance Nicholson where the same fly can be purchased and where it is now once again known as a Tout's Beige. Tying a size 16 onto my leader, I doubted whether such a small nondescript fly would be very visible on the water but needn't have worried. It stood up proudly and was quite distinctive against the dark water. However, it didn't rise a fish.

As I drifted further upstream the light drizzle increased to a thick, summer rain of the sort that soaks through everything. A short way above Hind's Pit, Hunting Bridge is a narrow crossing over the river constructed of metal girders, corrugated sheeting and concrete with rotten timbers dangling. A convenient rock, comfortably upholstered with thick moss, was quite dry under the bridge so I sat there to eat my breakfast muesli bar while soft rain fell on either side. A kingfisher made me smile as he drew an iridescent line of hope against the far bank.

Breakfast finished, I was too comfortable to move at once and, from where I sat, flicked the Beige lazily out into mid-stream. It landed no more than a couple of rod lengths out, bobbed towards me on the choppy current for a couple of feet and was accepted enthusiastically by a lively fish. Brightness swirled on the end of the line and came splashing to hand; a trout of lightest silver and gold, patterned with fine speckles and shining rings like raindrops on water. He was a plump eight inches – a perfect breakfast trout.

How pleasant it would have been to walk back to the Tarr Steps Hotel, to the welcoming scents of coffee and toast, and present my trout to the cook; to have him served in parsley butter with wild mushrooms and scrambled eggs, perhaps, and then to idle over coffee in the sitting room with the morning papers. But, however comfortable the stay, being a visitor would mean returning to urban life at the end of a week and how much nicer, really, to live close by and how privileged to enjoy kind invitations to visit this river whenever I wish. The trout also appeared satisfied with this arrangement, waving his tail briefly, as he slid serenely back to the cool stream.

.

CHAPTER 4

Foreign Invaders

By keeping two wheels in the hedge and holding his tummy in I hoped my vehicle could spend the day on the roadside near Withypool without causing too much obstruction. A convenient path leads to the river and continues all down the left bank so, equipped with rod and net, I followed its winding way through woodland, splattering across muddy places and clambering over rocky places, into the valley bottom.

Dew had not yet dried on the morning and no fish seemed yet to be rising in the cool, clear Barle. The first pool I reached appeared bottomless where dark water plunged over a rocky shelf so I tried a heavy bead-headed nymph to explore its depths but only succeeded in tugging tufts of moss from submerged rocks. I changed to a lighter nymph with a soft hackle and a red tag, one which would not sink so quickly, and felt a couple of tentative bites as the current swept it through the pool. Eventually I caught a dainty little salmon parr with a finely forked tail, smudgy bars marking his flanks, a black spot on each gill cover.

I wandered along the sunlit valley where woods and meadows sloped down on either side to the whispering, tree-cloistered river. Through the prism of whisky coloured water, stones of the riverbed appeared golden with here and there a paler one of quartz, but on dry beaches at the sides of the stream they all looked grey and I marvelled at how brightening water can be. In so many ways. Wagtails wagged their tails, dippers dipped courteously and a kingfisher flashed past in a blue electric spark.

A bird's pellet on a rock held pink fragments of shattered crayfish shell and nearby I found a whole dead crayfish, around three inches long. American signal crayfish have reached the River Barle by human introduction. They feed rapaciously on aquatic plants and invertebrates and take up residence in holes and crevices amongst rocks, driving small fish away from those places which are vital to hide from predators and, in times of spate, to find refuge from the hammering current. In an effort to understand more about them I had recently met Nicky Green, a crayfish scientist working on this river just upstream of Withypool.

Nicky had shown me where a long slice of riverbank had slipped out. The edge of about forty yards of bank lay in the river allowing water to wash behind it, forming a small back ditch. The exact shape and extent were difficult to see because both the severed strip and the bank behind it were obscured by the long leaves and orange flowers of montbretia, but as we walked through the riverside meadows we saw another similar length, and then another.

"This has happened because of the crayfish," Nicky had told me. She explained how they tunnel into riverbanks and showed me their burrows, with a flat base and a rounded top like a capital letter D on its back. Where crayfish are numerous the earth banks become perforated with hundreds of these holes close to the waterline. In times of spate the honeycombed earth is too unstable to stand against the scouring current so it crumbles into the water and the bank collapses.

"When we began this work there was hardly any montbretia here," Nicky said. "All this erosion has happened in the last five years and when bare soil is exposed the most aggressively colonising plant in the river takes advantage; in this location it is montbretia. The corms get washed downstream until they land in a patch of bare soil where they take root."

Nicky explained how erosion was changing the nature of the river, how crumbling earth banks clog the riverbed with silt and how the course of the river grows wider and shallower, allowing the current to slow and water temperature to rise, so the river holds less oxygen. A muddy, deoxygenated river would be quite unsuitable for most wildlife of a tumbling, freestone river like the Barle. Species that live here are adapted to cool, well oxygenated water bubbling over a clean, pebbly bed. Stoneflies, for example, whose larvae live underwater in cool rapid streams where the clean rushing water is rich in oxygen, will not live in a muddy river. If fish eggs fall into mud they fail through lack of oxygen. In order to breed successfully, fish such as trout and salmon need to cut their redds, the scooped out pits which hold their spawn, in a clean stony riverbed where their eggs can settle between pebbles washed in a bubbling oxygen-rich current. So changing the nature of the riverbed would have a devastating impact on the ecology of the River Barle, including its fish, and this middle stretch populated by crayfish holds important trout and salmon spawning grounds.

"In the first five years of this project we killed 16,115 crayfish," said Nicky, "and sterilised 2,659 males, hoping they might hold territories without breeding. If you want to keep on top of them you have to keep intensively trapping, but you never get the last one and if you relax the effort numbers soon rebound so you have to keep it up. Probably indefinitely."

This sounded irresolvable, and it might be, but Nicky tentatively described how perhaps a crayfish population could stabilise in a habitat with good numbers of large predators such as eels, pike and other bigger fish. I remembered gutting rainbow trout I had caught on the River Exe and finding signal crayfish claws in their stomachs. The concept of developing a population of larger fish in the rivers is an interesting idea but there is still so much to learn and so little time and I thought what terrible things crayfish are.

"They are not terrible in their place," Nicky had insisted.

"Yes, it is terrible that they're here, but humans have brought them." She had looked almost sympathetic as she added sadly, "It's not their fault."

As the day ripened the valley was suffused with sultry heat and at the lower end of a gorsey cleave, abuzz with grasshoppers and crickets, I came to Oakbeer Wood and the bottom of the beat. Below a spreading beech I sat on a mossy rock to eat some chocolate and change my nymph to a dry fly. Perhaps a Dulverton Destroyer might do the trick, I thought. And it did.

Dark clouds gathered in the north as I worked my way back upstream, casting into pools and pockets as I went and I winkled out half a dozen or so brown trout; small but pretty, they were all around four to six inches long. Then I reached a wide sweeping bend with shilletty pebbles on the inside, shaded by an elephantine grey-skinned beech from the far bank. At the spot where the stream emerged from beech-shadow a bramble hung over the bank, dangling its tip into the river at the tail of the pool, idly feeling the water, and just beside it a fish moved.

It was not easy to get below the spot to cast up to it as I should have liked to do, so I crouched at the side of the shilletty shallow and cast across the river, dropped my fly onto the dark water below the canopy and watched it glide along with the slow slide of the current. As it neared the bramble I saw that the line was too long, the fly was on course to pass it on the far side and the leader would wrap around its prickly stem. I waited as long as I dared, hoping the fish might rise before the fly became caught up. At the last second, the leader only an inch away from entanglement, I gave the line a quick twitch to pull the fly from danger. The fly made a little hop sideways and at the same moment it was snatched from the air by ravenous jaws.

The fish plummeted into the pool pulling line thrumming

into its depths, bending my rod into a respectful bow. Eventually I drew him in and as he slid over the rim of my net I admired a spotted silver fuselage, a bold eye and a nuggety nine inches of trout.

When I got back to my vehicle I took a flask of tea and piece of cake to sit on the cleave overlooking the river, my gaze passing small grass fields, soaring above the roofs of the village to the moors beyond. In the distance a tractor puttered around picking up hay bales but otherwise the only sound was the softly sighing river. As I finished the moist apple-and-almond cake an accomplished friend had made and drained my enamel mug the first drops of rain pattered around me and the rich scent of earth and flowers and grasses rose from the land, smudging the valley in a steamy cloud of petrichor.

CHAPTER 5

Barle Beauty

It had been a busy working afternoon, I had a late appointment at seven o'clock and it was already five when I decided that if I left now there might just be time to fish on the way. If I was quick. After all, I should be passing Marsh Bridge and a friend had kindly invited me to fish his water on the River Barle a little way upstream. It was sunny with an easterly breeze so conditions weren't ideal but there was birdsong and bee-hum and I would not stay long. Just for an hour, I thought. A selection of rods and waders were already in my vehicle where they live all summer, just in case. So off I went.

A muddy track leaves the tarmac road to wind through lofty woodland and as I trundled along it I met Charles, who lives there in a house on the riverbank. After lots of "Hello! How are you? How lovely to see you!"ing, Charles asked what I was doing there.

"Fishing."

"Oh, but my dear, there aren't any fish," Charles wailed. He went on to tell me how, when he was growing up, there would have been five, six or seven takeable trout of at least three quarters of a pound in every pool. "Every pool, I tell you," he insisted. "Some mornings I would lean over the rails of Marsh Bridge and see seven or eight beautiful trout below the bridge, and I knew it would be a good day. Now there are none. You go and look there now – you will not see a fish."

We turned off our engines, pulled on handbrakes and chatted through open widows in the relaxed local custom of vehicle-to-vehicle conversation. I asked what he thought had happened to the fish but Charles wasn't sure.

"Is it farming? I don't know," he wondered. But, I pointed out, there was no intensive farmland upstream; indeed nothing but woodland for miles then some fairly extensively managed pasture and then acres of moorland. There was no obvious source of pollution or problems but, we agreed, the life-force of the river was undeniably diminished.

"It's not just trout, it's everything," Charles went on. "Birds, frogs, I would say we have a tenth of the frogs we used to have. And insects. Everything has gone."

Insects create the broad base of nutrition in the interconnected web of life; they are vital in the diet of birds, fish, amphibians and small mammals and through pollination they are responsible for the production of fruit, berries and seeds and so for the perpetuation of many plants – there would be little for any of us to eat without insects. And insects, it is true, are disappearing. I remember summers when splattered insects had to be cleaned off car windscreens after every drive; when an open window and a light switched on at night filled a room with moths; when parties of flies spun below the ceiling and died on the windowsill in every room. Old fishermen remember summer evenings when insects over a river darkened the air in a cloud wider than its banks and higher than the trees stretching for the length of the river in unimaginable abundance. There has been so much loss.

"Do you know, I'm 83, I've known this part of the Barle since I was a boy, and it's dying." Charles shook his head sadly, clearly distressed by the river's fortunes.

This was discouraging but whilst I believed all Charles told me, I would not be deterred from my plan. Though the fortunes of fish may be grim, surely they could not have gone altogether.

A little further up the valley I parked on the riverbank, pulled on thigh waders as those were the quickest and decided I mustn't be long. The water was clear and faintly golden so that, except in bubbling turbulence, there was a good view of dark rock and golden pebbles below, yet nowhere could I see any fish. However, it was shady under the trees, the east wind had been left behind and air in this sheltered valley was almost still. Only the river rushed.

A 1930s *Where To Fish* guide published by *The Field* magazine assures visiting fishermen of good trouting to be had on the Exe and Barle around Dulverton and that fish averaging four to the pound may be expected. So perhaps trout of about four ounces were the norm even then, though I don't doubt there were bigger ones among them.

Fish are indicators of the health of a river and it is worryingly clear that both sizes and numbers of fish are diminishing as rivers suffer many human imposed pressures. Some of the reasons appear obvious, including pollution from agriculture and sewage discharges which increase in incidence and concentration as the river runs its course. It is less clear why problems persist higher upstream in stretches where there is little or no source of contamination.

Yet for me as an angler, the size of fish is less important than their wildness. If catching large fish was my priority I should not be fishing rivers at all but well-stocked stillwaters. It is good, occasionally, to feel something hefty bending my rod and have something to take home for supper, but fishing a river is a different experience and its joy is not in the size of fish but in stepping into a wild place to interact with a wild fish in its own environment, on its own terms. Success depends upon observation and the quality of our attentiveness in watching, listening, feeling the water. This kind of fishing is not about hauling out large trout, but is more about a quiet conversation with a river.

The River Barle hastened along between the oaks of Draydon Wood and steep conifer clad slopes of Shircombeslade. Fishing here was tricky. I had picked up a ten foot rod based on the width of the river but trees stretching their gnarled limbs over the water were lower than I had appreciated and, in fact, a shorter rod might have been better. A spot with a fast, deep run between rocks close under the near bank looked enticingly fishy but my inexpert casting was not equal to it and as I ventured out towards mid-stream the current quickly became too deep and strong to go far. I followed what looked like a path along the bank, leaping from stone to stone, stepping over roots, glad of the blanketing moss for a little grip. The path grew progressively narrower, the bank steeper, effectively cutting me off from the track which was now high above my head and before I found anywhere with space to cast a fly it petered out altogether. It was frustratingly slow to retrace my clambering steps all the way back to the track; I was irritatingly conscious of time and fishing never works if you're in a hurry.

At Draydon Ford the river was easily accessible and as I waded over the shallow crossing a girl on a chestnut horse came from the opposite bank shouting a cheery greeting as we passed in mid-stream. I had a few casts across the river but there were no good pools within reach, though it was encouraging to see lots of little fry in the shallows; they were the only fish I had seen. Worried about being late, I nearly gave up at that point, feeling incompetent and rushed, but checked the time on my phone (which I had brought for that purpose alone – there was no signal for phone calls) and decided I might stay just a few minutes longer.

So I crossed the river and walked down the left bank. There was no track but the land was level there and a tractor working with timber, it seemed, had flattened the dense bracken and undergrowth leaving a temporary path through the wood. I followed his wheel marks, waders flumping at every step, and managed to reach the river opposite the deep run that had looked so good from the far bank. A shallow, pebbly beach on this side made access much easier.

Overarching trees seemed high and spacious but that was deceptive and I soon lost a gold headed black nymph to a down-swept beech branch. I tied on a different nymph. It was small, about a size fourteen, a twist of black peacock herl with a little red tag at the tail and the tiniest white tag at the head, like an emerging nymph.

With few roll casts towards the far bank, I let the nymph swing around in the fast current, then waded out far enough to cast upstream towards the head of the pool. There was no sudden take, no twitching rod tip or dipping leader, just a growing awareness of weight. When I lifted the rod it bowed double and I realised there was a decent sized fish on. He was too dignified for splashing or floundering; I reeled in against a steady resistance and, as his silvery length circled the pool below me, drew a long intake of breath. This was a beautiful fish. When he came to hand he was dark bronze mottled with pewter, his garnet-studded flanks a brassy gold and his belly silver. I should think he might have weighed three quarters of a pound. Naturally, I addressed him with great respect, almost apologising for disturbing his afternoon but explained that I was delighted, truly, to make his acquaintance and, as he slid back into the enfolding current, told him I was so very glad to know he was there.

Fishing is best done at leisure, of course, with a picnic and time to lounge on the bank amid a whole summer day of idling and dreaming. But even an hour snatched from a hectic working day can bring light to a dull soul, joy to a freedom-starved heart: an hour on a river is a glimpse of heaven.

The River Heddon

CHAPTER 6

Exploring the Heddon

The Heddon is a wild, rocky river plunging to the sea down a sharply chiselled valley, austere in line, profile and stony aspect, where the steep brackeny cleaves are sometimes torn with loose scree and sometimes comforted with sessile oak woodland, though even that cowers low, hard pruned by sea-borne gales.

I persuaded Chris to come along with me; a great fishing companion, he always brings a hip flask, lets me use his rods which are far better quality than mine and, most importantly, he knows how to catch fish. We parked near Hunter's Inn and walked the easy path through woodland, down to the surf-hammered, pigeon-grey pebble and boulder beach. Tide was high and the sun bright.

A relentless violence of tides has flung pebbles ashore and swept them into a bar, mounded along the top of the wave-washed beach, blockading the mouth of the river. At low to moderate flow river water filters through the bar, finding its way between pebbles and emerging just below the tideline to join the clear green ocean. In times of spate water spills over the top and a really heavy flood breaches the stony bar for a while; it is only then that salmon and peal, or sea trout, can get in or out of the river – at other times it is effectively closed to migrating fish.

Claude Wade, staying at Lynton, used to have to guess whether there had been enough rain to open the river and bring the peal up; often he miscalculated and had to be content with a day's trout fishing. Chris and I would be extremely satisfied with a day's trout fishing and had set out with just that intention; I had never caught a salmon or a peal anyway and would be perfectly delighted with a little brown trout. The narrow beach is wedged between jagged broken-toothed cliffs and Wade wrote encouragingly of, even here, generally getting a trout or two among the stones.

Well, we tried. The first few pools looked inviting and banks cut from bare rock offered a clear back cast but an east wind funnelling down the valley tossed the light line back into our faces. We took turns with a seven foot six rod but, despite several changes of fly, those first promising looking pools produced nothing and as we moved upstream it became clear that the Heddon trout were not to be taken lightly. At length a fish rose to examine my Deer Hair Sedge but didn't actually take the fly. Still, it was encouraging to know there were fish here and we had interested one. I was to 'interest' several more before the end of the day.

After half a mile or so, still fishless, we sat on the bank in the sun, ate some chocolate and wondered at the trickiness of Heddon trout and the strange stark beauty of this narrow valley – stony hills towering to sky on either side and the vibrant stream hurtling between rocks, rushing towards the sea.

Fishing the Heddon was hard. Wade had pointed out that beyond a mile upstream from the sea casting a fly would be almost impossible and on most of the river it was necessary to fish with a worm, yet even for that you would have to be pretty good at working your bait in amongst bushes. There was considerably less than a mile before shelter from salt winds allowed the banks to become overgrown with willow, alder and oak, severely restricting casting. However, we were not to be led astray by Wade's recommendation of a worm. Scrambling through bushes, strangled by brambles, we changed to a six foot rod and employed a folding hand saw in more than one place to open a little elbow room.

Eventually we reached a more open pool on a wide bend where tiny flies trailing long tails rose over the stream on translucent, fluttering wings. There was nothing to match them in my fly tin but Chris produced a beautifully delicate fly tied with a mole-fur dubbed body, a light grey hackle and three strands of fine monofilament as tails. It looked perfect.

The leafy canopy cast dark dappled shade pierced by brilliant spots of sun, the water's surface shattered into mirror-like shards and foamed with bubbles – it was almost impossible to see the tiny fly. Nevertheless, in the pool above the footbridge Chris caught a beautiful plump trout, silver sided and brightly spotted; around nine inches of wild Exmoor fizz.

We continued to work our way upstream, crossing and re-crossing the tumultuous river to find a way along. Although only a few paces wide, the water was fast and strong so I was often glad of overhanging branches to help me across. In places we had to climb onto the banks, pushing through smothering bracken and snaring bramble to pass rapids and falls where water boiled white between rocks.

When the valley bottom spread wide enough to accommodate it, a small meadow nestled between the woods steeping up on either side. The sward was coarse and tussocky with cocksfoot, meadowsweet, clumps of rushes and tangles of bracken and appeared very little grazed though nibbled bramble shoots showed it was browsed by deer.

We passed over several stretches where low boughs of oak and ash raked the water but, here and there, found little fishable pools in between. In one of these I lost sight of the fly amongst rapids and reflections but thought I saw the smallest splash of a fish and almost felt the faintest twitch on my line. It was more luck than skill but I was delighted to bring to hand my first Heddon trout; only a few inches long but zippy as the dashing stream. Chris produced his shot flask and we toasted our success of a fish each. A small success, perhaps, but they were hard-won fish in tricky conditions.

We had almost reached the hotel and the valley softened with meadows where cattle waded through tall grasses and fritillaries floated among flowers. I was blissfully unaware of time, as I always am when fishing, and was completely taken aback when Chris announced that it was four o'clock and time to go.

This river is testing of both skill and patience and we had to respect Mr Wade's success with both trout and peal. We did not see any salmon or peal, unsurprisingly as the river mouth was closed with pebbles at the beach, yet even without them and supposing I had been clever enough to hook all the half dozen or so fish I rose we could not have hoped to compete with Wade's catch. He recorded trout of excellent size and condition, sometimes up to a pound or even more in weight, and considered a good basket to comprise three or four good peal and from twenty to thirty trout. Today the River Heddon can be fished under the Westcountry Angling Passport Scheme and catch reports on the website show records of a one, a zero, a three and a respectable thirteen. (I wonder who achieved that?) Anyway, there is nothing approaching twenty to thirty.

So what has gone wrong? My own modest catch might be put down to an unimpressive performance, but Chris's certainly could not and it is unlikely to be a failure of all four rods whose catches were recorded online. The river had its unfishable stretches a hundred years ago, just as it has today and I don't think Mr Wade can have spent very much longer on the river than we did that day as he writes of enjoying lunch or tea at the hotel – a luxury we did not make time for. Perhaps worms would have been more productive than flies, but I think it most likely that the fish are simply not there in the numbers they used to be. This conclusion is supported by recent Environment Agency surveys which found numbers of eel, stoneloach, salmon and brown trout all failed to reach the threshold for 'good' quality.

The stretch of the River Heddon we fished, between Hunter's Inn and the sea, has no roads, buildings or commercial agriculture along its banks, only woodland, scree and a couple of intermittently grazed small meadows. But what of the water above; could this clear torrent of crystal foaming from the moors be carrying invisible impurities within it? One day I set off to explore.

* * *

Above Hunter's Inn, the little river comes down between steep woodlands with tiny meadows nestling in the bottom and is followed by a narrow road, twisting between fern-fringed hedgebanks, overhung by ash, oak and sycamore. Names such as Mill Farm, Mill Town and Mill Wood remember that the power of this stream was once harnessed for industry but today, its work finished, it is allowed to run its heedless way. After about a mile, the road swings away to higher land and a footpath follows the course of the river. Gradually, as the valley becomes less steep, woods give way to sheep-nibbled grass fields and eventually the village of Parracombe.

In the middle of the village I leaned over the bridge railings to watch the river pass and noticed a tiny bird hopping about in a garden conifer growing over the wall. A wren, I thought, but its movement was not quite right for a wren and looking closer I saw it was a goldcrest – such a bright surprise, like a gleam of sunlight on a grey day.

On its way through the village the river is kept under strict control, confined between stone walls fitted with occasional sets of steps where the good folk of Parracombe would have collected water and the gaping ends of drainage pipes where they would have returned it, and perhaps still do. Even this apparently pristine river must act as a drain for human waste, it was not hard to find pipes spewing out foul smelling grey sludge; and though the few houses the river passes have increased little in number over the past century, the quantity and virulence of chemicals we all regularly dispose of has.

Yet it seems pollution is not this river's only problem. Due to the steep landform it inhabits, falling from 1,230 feet to the sea in around four and a half miles, the Heddon is a fast spatey river; in lower reaches small gravel is regularly scoured out, only substantial rocks having sufficient weight to resist the power of the current, and it would be almost impossible for aquatic plants to gain a root hold in the rolling riverbed. These conditions do not make good trout spawning habitat. If fish do manage to spawn here, their eggs are likely to be washed out of the gravel in winter floods and fry could be swept away from safe nursery areas. However, in the headwaters above Parracombe flow is more regular, there are some excellent patches of fine gravel suitable for spawning and weed growth offers safer areas with food and cover for young fry. Trout in the lower reaches may have migrated downstream from these headwater breeding grounds.

The tendency for dramatically varying flow causes considerable variation in the population of each new generation of fish, success being highly dependent on rainfall with juvenile numbers likely to be low after a winter of deluges. The river's steep gradient is nothing new, but perhaps the pattern of rainfall is. As more moisture is drawn up into clouds by warmer air, climate change is increasing the occurrence of heavy rainstorms and it seems this situation is likely to worsen in the coming years.

Above the village, the River Heddon is blessed by water issuing from two holy wells, St Thomas's Well and Lady's Well. I sat beside Lady's Well for a while, watching water bubble fresh from pale pebbles between emerald clumps of cress and spurge. This mysterious water upwelling from the ground may have been held deep within the earth for years, possibly centuries, out of sight and mind and beyond the reach of people where perhaps it had escaped contamination by any of our foul discharges. I could not know its origin but it tasted clean, mineral, cold. This newly minted water ran below an old ash moote and cascaded between ferns, below hazels and withies festooned in honeysuckle, and went dancing away to join the river.

The young River Heddon is gathered from numerous small streams issuing from high moorland between Parracombe and Challacombe. From Rowley Down, Highley, Tennerdy and Holworthy many tiny trickles contribute their strength to the growing torrent. Exploring its highest beginnings I walked over tussocky bog, only possible in the unusually dry weather, where desiccated mosses were faded colourless as winter moor grass. At the head of Highley a tea coloured runnel draining from the bog cut deep into peaty soil, its tinny voice echoing hollowly around the chamber it carved for itself as it curled like a foetus growing into a new river in the dark belly of the moor.

A low guttural cough echoed across the combe as the lead hind of a strung-out group barked a rebuke from the opposite cleave; a clear accusation of trespass into territory where humans were not expected or welcome. The deer moved downhill, through a tall beech fence to drop into cover, heading the same way as the gurgling stream as it slid over shilletty stone lit by late sunlight glowing through the amber prism of peaty water. I looked out to the distant coast and to the shining meeting of sea and sky between Hartland Point and the far off hills of Wales, where rounded headlands of Lundy Island were silhouetted by slanting rays in a dazzling crystallisation of light and water: the ultimate destination of this exuberant moorland stream.

The River Lyn and its Tributaries

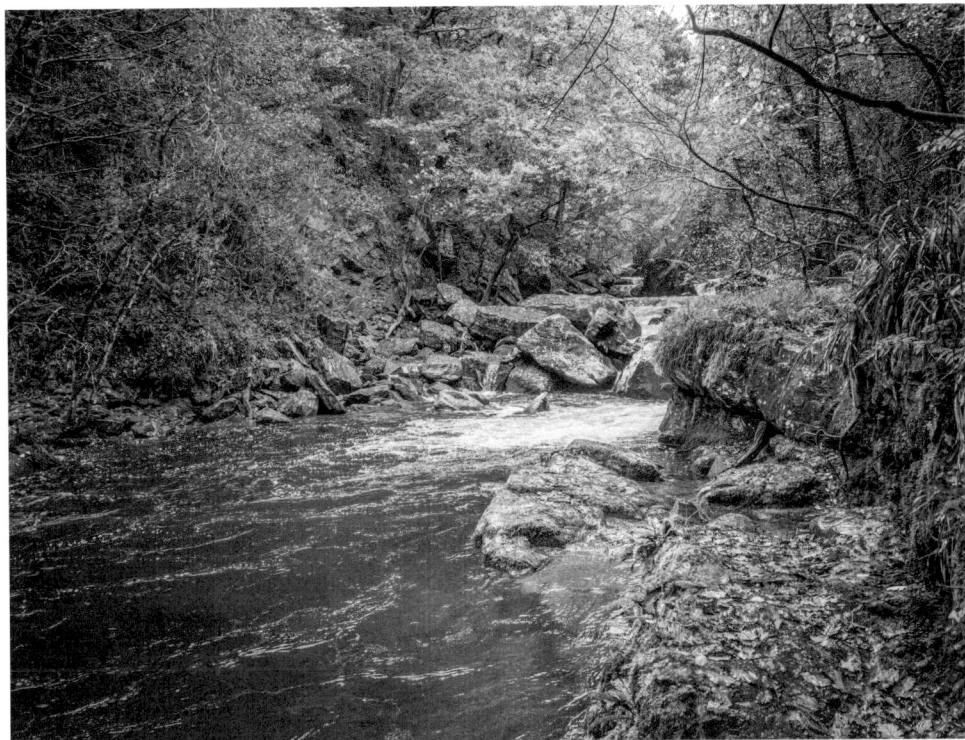

CHAPTER 7

Farley Water

———

Farley Water is small and rocky, fast and wild as the little brown trout who live there. Beginning on Exe Plain it wriggles its way across Brendon Common, dashing along to join the waters of the Lyn on their way to the sea. As it goes it cuts a seam of white water and grey stone into the richly coloured moorland where green and tan bracken and purple heather is flecked with the gold of western gorse.

On a warm but overcast morning I parked near Dry Bridges from where the hills of moorland, like swelling waves, roll into the south. Travelling light, I carried my rod over my shoulders on an improvised sling made of baler cord and elastic bands and walked down the little combe between Middle Hill and Farley Hill, where sheep grazed amongst bracken, thorn and mountain ash trees, and down to the boundary fence at the end of Brendon Common, which encloses the in-bye land of Farley Water Farm.

From there I followed the stream, working my way up the water, stopping here and there to cast a fly into each pool that looked in any way hopeful. Most were really very small. In several pools I happily managed to put my little fly exactly where I thought it should go yet still got no response. I began to wonder whether there were any fish in this little stream, but couldn't really believe there were not.

Below sheltering birch and mountain ash, a narrow pool was deeply wedged into a fissure of rock and I sat on the bank to cast into it. The fly was met by the quick splip of a rise but my strike failed to connect. Despite reproaching my slowness I was pleased to have found a fish and determined to try again. I knew I should really change the fly, offer something that looks different, but didn't want to because I had no other fly that would show up so well on the dark, bubbling current as this little Adams with its orange post. So I sat for a while, ate some chocolate and dressed the fly with floatant powder hoping to at least change the way it sat on the water.

After a few minutes I cast into the pool again and watched the fly slowly twire around on an eddy that carried it towards the sheer rock wall. Splip! and I missed again. How could I be so incompetent, so slow, so stupid, so thoroughly useless?

I retrieved the fly, dried it off and put down the rod, pulled some lunch from my pocket and bit into apple and nuts in self-disgust. I knew I should leave this pool and move on but this was the first fish I had seen, the first rise I had induced and in my stubborn, unreasonable obstinacy determined to try again. I only ate half my lunch – too impatient, you see, and I knew he would never rise to the same fly a third time.

But he did!

As I raised the rod to strike I lifted the fish clear out of the water, such was his weightless littleness, and swung him into the pool below where he came off and sparkled away into the chuckling current and I was happy, at last, to let him go. I'm not sure which of us my laughter was for.

Farley Water is the stream where Wade, as a small boy, first learned to fish, using a stick of a rod with the line tied to one small ring at the top and a worm, hunting out about a dozen little troutlets from under the banks and rocky holes. He tells us that, without doubt, Farley Water and Combe Park Water produce the smallest fish on the moor.

In 1902 the Lynmouth Association, Wade tells us, restricted

the size of fish to be kept to no less than six inches which on the main river he considered reasonable but went on to say that 'such a limitation would never do on the small streams, for I undertake to say that a man might catch fifty trout in a day up Farley Water, and that if this rule as to size were strictly carried out he would have to throw every one of them back again.'

I was content that my fish be little ones, I planned to return them all to the stream anyway, but felt quite certain I should never be able to catch fifty in a day, and wondered again how much that was due to my inexperience as a fisherman and how much to the numbers of fish in the stream. Both numbers and sizes of fish are determined by the quality of the stream they inhabit and especially by the supply of food they can find there. Exmoor streams are a harsh environment, the loose stones of their bed mobile and unstable in the flashy, spatey current; rainfall on the nearby Chains is almost eighty inches a year. High altitude and exposed locations lead to extremes of temperature – icy and wind blasted in winter, shallow and shadeless in summer. It is little wonder that species of invertebrates sufficiently adapted for survival here are limited. Yet this moorland, grazed by cattle, sheep and ponies, appears hardly changed in hundreds of years. If a basket of fifty trout in a day was normal a century and a half ago, I saw no reason why it should not be today.

It started to rain and I did not like the thought of getting drenched; Exmoor weather can be unpredictable, smiling one minute and snarling the next. So I found a comfortable dry spot amongst the moss-upholstered roots of an old beech and sat there to finish my lunch watching raindrops stipple the pool ahead. A little band of brown flies came to join me. They were not troublesome at all and did not show any interest in either my skin or my lunch but seemed only to be seeking shelter from the rain, resting on dry moss protected by the leafy beech canopy, as I was.

The shower passed and the flies and I emerged to resume our day. On the next big bend the outside bank was deeply scoured,

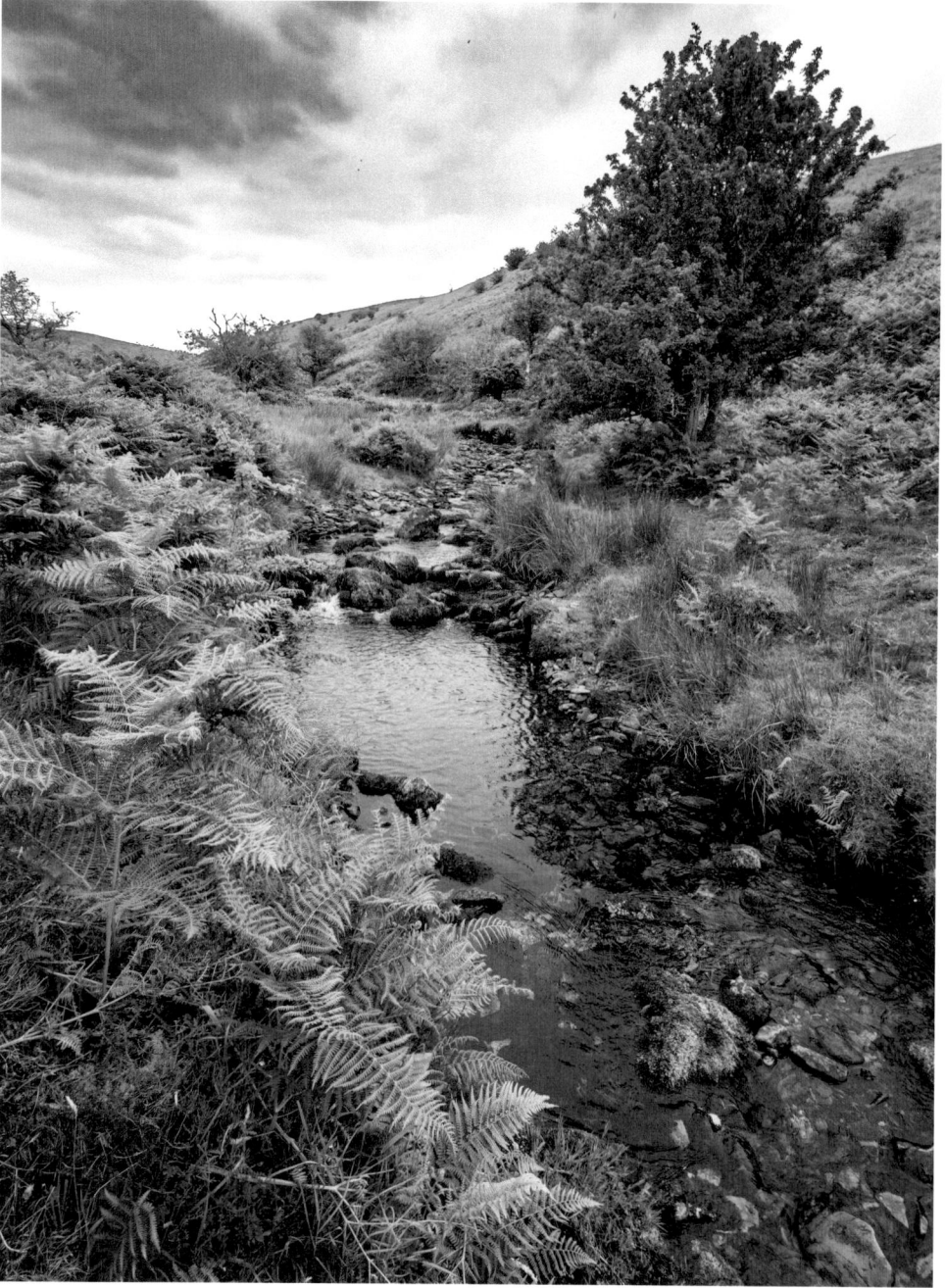

exposing a vertical profile of soil the colour of a dun horse, studded with stone and topped with a black layer of peat. On this cliff face the ghost of a nest was outlined in moss and moor grass, hollow and empty as an eggshell, long abandoned but a reminder that this wild spot was once chosen by a couple of birds, probably dippers I thought, as home to raise their brood. It would not have been an easy place to feed a family – I hope they succeeded. At the bank's foot a tarry mass of fish bones melted over a rock showed where an otter had regularly passed. His presence was encouraging – he had clearly found plenty of fish here.

A little further upstream a small thorn tree crouched over a pool, its roots running along the edge of the bank like basketwork, weaving together earth, moss, stone, heather; and on the trailing tip of one fine root like an extended finger grew a delicate sprig of tormentil with yellow flowers. I cast below the thorn a couple of times. Nothing. So I crept forward and sat on a rock opposite the little tree to cast further up the pool. On the second cast I contacted a fish. Lively as a weasel, he darted rapidly about the pool, drawing line through the water like a blade. He was a darkly spotted seven inches, highlighted with scarlet.

After holding him in the water to admire his splendour I let him slip back to the chuckling stream, and as I sat on the bank eating a handful of sharp-sweet whortleberries and a little chocolate I gazed at the moorland hills around me coated in broad swathes of heather, bracken and moor grass, dotted with thorn bushes, while high overhead a buzzard floated circles in the dreaming sky.

So the little stream led me along until I came to a big mound in the valley bottom the map names Alse Barrow, though it appeared more of a natural feature than a man made barrow. Perhaps it is both. Where Farley Water passes this protuberance its course is deeper, secluded by steeper land either side, and in its shelter there are more trees – thorn, willow and mountain ash. The cleave opposite was vibrant with deep purple bell heather chiming with yellow gorse, honeysuckle and ivy flowers attracted bees and hoverflies and a pair of white butterflies waltzed on a light breeze.

In the narrow course between high banks the only way to get a fly onto the water was to drop it down from above. I doubted it would work but, eternally optimistic as all fishermen must be, I had to try anyway. So I lay on the grassy bank, peered over the edge and dangled the line between tufts of bracken and heather. The fly touched the water and floated down a few yards before it was received with a lively sploop and when I flicked up the rod the fish landed on the bank beside me. Laughing, I scooped him up at once and dropped him back into the water. Another small one but bright as the golden tormentil spangling the bank.

Wade writes of how, in the past, he caught baskets of eighty and of a hundred fish in this water, though they were little ones. And whilst I could not hope to reach numbers such as those, I completely agree when he says, 'I absolutely deny that the standard of Exmoor fishing is to be measured by the measurement of its fish.'

The afternoon was wearing on and I had a fair walk back over the common so, content with my 'basket' decided to finish. As I dismantled my rod and looped elastic bands around to sling it across my back the sun came out, and as I walked up over Pig Hill, away from the stream, the constant chatter of water receded allowing the whole audioscape of the wide moor to open around me like hills coming into focus when a fog lifts. With the stream only a distant shush I could hear sheep calling, a passing crow, a conversation of ravens and the gentle west wind carrying a honeyed scent of heather whispering through the grass.

CHAPTER 8

Hoaroak Water

———

The cleave above Blackpits Bridge somehow manages to be both steep and boggy at once but I scrambled up, sinking to my ankles here and there in sloppy black peat, circled around the shoulder of Dure Down and followed the fence line, wading through rushes and moor grass, to Exe Head. The nascent River Exe trickled away to the east but I set off northwards along a better trodden path where red and black cattle grazed contentedly on the hill. After a little way, Short Chains Combe came gurgling in on my left and from there onwards the cheerful chattering of waters kept me company all day.

A valley cuts sharply into moorland between The Chains to the west and Exe Plain to the east, where tussocky rushes and sedges give the land a wiry pelt and here and there coppery fronds of bracken drift between seeding grasses. The Chains is a high, boggy tract of quaking land and draining from it down the deep Long Chains Combe, where a pleated series of headlands unfolds, comes the beginnings of Hoaroak Water.

A burnished bronze slow worm stretched across the path and I picked him up to remove him from danger of trampling. Reptiles are vulnerably lethargic on cool mornings, and often visit stony paths in search of sun to quicken their bodies. He twisted through my fingers, his smooth, muscular coils gripping my hand briefly like a friend before I let him slip away into a safer lie among the rushes.

As I walked on down the sheltered track following the water, the day began to warm and cattle and sheep retreated to patches of shade below thorn bushes and in narrow goyles etched into the north facing hillside. In a little way I came to an oak tree on the right bank, protected from the ravages of teeth and antlers by a plain post and rail enclosure.

The Hoar Oak Tree is a famous and important tree, marking the boundaries of Devon and Somerset and the meeting point of the Forest of Exmoor, Lynton Common and Brendon Common. Until John Knight bought the newly inclosed Forest in 1819 and built a wall around it, such features as notable trees, barrows and stones were relied upon to define boundaries, to mark the spot, to form, quite literally, landmarks. It is a nicely shaped if small, somewhat stunted oak and was rooted here to replace an earlier tree, which itself had stood in the place of one blown down in a storm on Boxing Day 1916, and that one may have succeeded the great tree which fell 'with very age and rottenness' in about 1658. I imagine that ancient tree must have been of massive girth, probably hollow and hoary with epicormic growth bristling from its bark; and I wonder whether a yet earlier oak stood on the site before it, but human memory cannot stretch so far and no one seems to know. The present tree, though of unimpressive appearance, carries the proud office of this ancient lineage – even the stream is named after it.

Hoaroak Water runs along the western edge of Brendon Common, between Cheriton Ridge and the steep flank of Furzehill Common, then on below Cheriton, Scoresdown and Combe Park, where it assumes the name of Combe Park Water, to join Farley Water at Hillsford Bridge and the East Lyn at Watersmeet. It is a merry little stream, bubbling and chuckling as it goes.

Wade refers to the fishing records of a friend who, he tells us, on fifteen occasions between 1871 and 1889, caught between sixty and a hundred trout in Farley Water and Hoaroak Water, and five times caught over a hundred. They were small, however, averaging no better than twelve to the pound, though no fish was kept under three and a half inches in length, the largest fish being half a pound.

The summer morning unfolded as I walked down the moorland valley and then turned to fish back upstream, casting into little pools here and there, seeing plenty of fish but finding them difficult to catch in the low, clear water. In one spot the valley opened out on my left, into a flat area, wet and rushy, pooled and pondweeded, dribbling slowly into the stream. Here, from the shade of the north-facing left bank a little trout parr accepted my size fourteen Adams and came splashily to hand. He was small, as Mr Wade had warned he might be, but brightly marked with big, baby eyes and three rows of scarlet spots across his flanks. When I released him he squiggled away in delight and then, with the peace that comes from the satisfaction of even such a small success when any success is doubtful, I sat on the stream bank to eat some lunch.

Hoaroak Water tumbles along in a series of low falls, fast riffles and some surprisingly deep pools, and where bracken and gorse allowed I cast a fly under the bank or into the bubble line and caught a couple more trout. In one spot a conveniently positioned stone at the tail of a pool made an ideal place to sit while I cast up towards white water at the pool's head. In another, I stretched out on sheep-nibbled grass below a thorn tree to dangle my line over the bank into water a few feet below. In places the valley floor widened into streamy, trickling networks of runnels weaving between wide, shallow pools where mud carried slots of hinds and padding of a fox. Everywhere the land smelled of crushed bracken and late summer grasses, small olives danced over the water and warm August sunshine dripped like syrup.

Just above the stream, Hoar Oak Cottage is little more than a ruined shell sitting low on the hillside. It must have been one

of the most remote shepherd's dwellings on Exmoor, never having electricity, piped water or sewerage, and not even served with a track. Moorland has now reclaimed the little enclosures that were once held safely between hedges; all that remains are low banks, the hedgerow beech grown up into trees. Small clusters of nettles show where the land was once enriched with dung – the soil there remembering a house cow, a few hens, a pony. Spleenwort sprouts from the mortar of roofless, grass-topped walls where doorways, windows, fireplaces remain open portals through which ghosts can wind around the stone remains; and I wondered whose eyes once gazed through them daily, whose hand rested on the sill.

One of the past inhabitants, James Maxwell Johnstone, was a Scottish shepherd employed to manage the Hoar Oak herding. In 1886 he and his wife Sarah came to live in this shepherd's cott where they raised thirteen children. Water came from a nearby spring, meals were cooked over a peat fire and washing was done in the stream.

A cubby hole on one side of the fireplace is filled with a generous nest of twigs and moss, I thought probably a blackbird's, and inside the smoke blackened chimney swallows have built a mud-walled bowl – so children, of sorts, are still raised within the shelter of these walls.

Just below Hoar Oak ruins, where the stream wends its way through the gorse, there is a nice little pool and I wondered whether those long-ago souls might have fished it. I'm sure they did. They might not have used a fly rod, I expect tickling or 'groping' was more their style, but they certainly would have winkled out a few trout for supper now and again.

It called for a fairly accurate cast to avoid spiky gorse pointing out from either side but I successfully sent my fly up to the top of the pool and was just feeling pleased with myself for avoiding the bushes when the land rumbled as if with a barrage of underground gunfire. A troop of dark moorland ponies came cantering down to the stream, a sea of black manes waved over their hammer-marked brown bodies, sturdy legs pounding the earth. They trampled snorting into the pool above me and sank pale muzzles into the cool water. Of course, I caught nothing there after that but could not object to their drinking.

A little further upstream a small tributary comes tumbling between mossy banks into a pool shaded by beech boughs. The two streams pause upon meeting, as though taking time to shake hands before setting off together as one, and in this junction pool a fish was rising. I crept as close as I dared but there was no cover so I kept low, curled on grey river-washed stones and cast towards the rings splooping intermittently under the beech. By some chance, my little fly managed to avoid the gorse threatening my back cast, sailed safely under the branches and landed in just the right spot to be greeted instantly with the rapid splash of a rise. I lifted the rod sharply but the fly came back to me apologetically, with no fish attached. Had I been too slow, too fast or did he not really take it? I wasn't sure but was vexed with myself, nevertheless.

I took a deep breath, ate some chocolate and changed the fly. I offered him two more flies but he wouldn't look at them. Nothing would induce him to rise again. The Hoar Oak trout may be small but they are very wily and to this one I had to admit defeat, but only for today; I would come back another time and try again, I determined, the Hoar Oak trout had not seen the last of me yet.

CHAPTER 9

Oare Water

A small fragment of purple gleamed amongst the grass, so vibrantly intense, so richly glossy it appeared less a part of the natural world and more a fabulous jewel. It was alive! As I watched, the butterfly stretched out the creases in his wings and I realised he must have only recently emerged, shiny and new, unfolding from a chrysalis lying below last year's dead oak leaves to become a creature of air. The glorious wings closed to display their underside, a discreet and rather distinguished silver grey finely etched in white, with one small orange spot dotted with a black pupil. He fluttered onto my hand, clasping my skin with pale slender legs but, to my disappointment, kept his wings firmly closed.

A purple hairstreak butterfly is purple as a kingfisher is blue: more light than pigment, more astonishment than appearance, a thing seeming more of heaven than of earth. They are seldom seen because most of their adult lives are spent fluttering about the top-most canopies of oak trees where they feed on honeydew secreted by aphids. This one seemed to be male as the females have only a splash of purple on otherwise dark wings. He allowed me one more brief glimpse of his improbable purple as he flew away.

Mike and Molly's meadows nestle below ancient oak wood-land pouring thickly over the hillside. At the bottom of the wood trees spread their canopies across a track, their branches stretching over the hedge and reaching out into the meadows beyond with an offer of shade for cattle. This meeting of woodland and grassland is rich in insect life and, as I walked, a buzz of flies swarmed around my head and pestered over my face. Some were horseflies, eager for blood, attacking any exposed skin so I rolled down my sleeves but they got the backs of my hands. Extraordinarily invincible for creatures so small, I soon gave up the hopeless task of swatting at them. And I remembered how, years ago, flies used regularly to be this thick but are seldom present in such numbers nowadays which, unpleasant as they can be, is rather worrying. Perhaps not so invincible as they seem.

Rawcombe Farm is neither large nor intensively managed and Mike and Molly take a relaxed attitude to agriculture, as to most other aspects of life. They are always ready for a chat and always have amusing tales to tell.

Molly told me how she grew up in Porlock, where she learned from her older brother to tickle trout in the little stream that comes down from Hawk Combe. Molly in turn taught this skill to all her children as a useful means of procuring a meal. Her son Martin proved particularly adept and one day, fancying trout for lunch, he went down to the stream below the farm to hoik out half a dozen. He caught four but the trout of Oare Water are not large so he went back into the river looking for a couple more to make a good meal. Something drew his attention to the bank where he had lain his trout, lined up neatly on the grass, and there were only three. His brow furrowed. Surely he had caught four? He questioned whether his memory or his mathematics were at fault and was still puzzling over it when he spotted a small, black face watching him beadily from behind a mossy log. It was a mink! The cheeky culprit appeared to be awaiting an opportunity to repeat his crime so the trout were hastily removed to a safer place.

I wandered through meadows spreading kindly between the

hillside woodland and the banks of Oare Water. This stream comes into being from the meeting of Weir Water with Chalk Water and meanders through Oare and Malmsmead where it is joined by Badgworthy Water to become the East Lyn. Although small, it is a rocky rushing river; winter torrents from the nearby moor have driven deep gullies and gouged a twisting channel into bedrock as water carves its way through the land. Even in the low flow of summer this stream, narrow enough in places to reach across with my six foot rod, has pools too deep to venture and runnels too strong to broach. Yet many parts are clear and shallow with hardly a ripple to break the surface. I dared not approach the bank as, at my first glimpse of water, darting shadows sped away. The fish were wild and wary as deer and I could not get near them.

I slipped quietly into a pool which I knew fish had already vacated but upstream, in the green shade of a sycamore, rings of a rising fish dimpled the water. I waited quietly, hoping it would happen again and it did. So I prepared my fly – a pale Deer Hair Sedge to show up well on the dark stream. There was not much space between the water surface and the overhanging sycamore so a flat side cast was required to place the fly accurately at a fair distance without splashing or catching in the tree. I doubted my ability but determined to try.

My first cast went into the sycamore. I crept carefully out to retrieve it and returned to my station under the bank. On my second attempt the back cast caught in twigs of a fallen branch lying in the water downstream. I slowly moved down, patiently untied it, and inched back into position. My third cast went up the stream quite nicely and the fly landed softly, deep in the shade under the low tree, just where I wanted it. But it was too late by then; the fish knew I was there and would not consider my fly. There were no more rises. I tried a couple more casts with no real hope before clambering up the bank to try another spot.

As I worked my way up the meadows the stream became more sharply incised into rock so the banks were high, open runs were very shallow and clear and deeper pools heavily over-hung with trees. Perhaps, I thought, I might have done better by cutting back a few branches first. I clambered about trying a cast here and a cast there but could not catch a fish.

I sat on the bank, watched the stream and ate some chocolate. I was vexed with my ineptitude and found little comfort in remembering that even Wade had found this stretch difficult as the stream was heavily overgrown and the banks high, so nothing much has changed, and he often walked up the road to miss it out. It was frustrating but I tried to relax (I am not good at relaxing in the face of failure and tension only makes my fish-ing worse) and to take consolation in the beautiful landscape and glorious weather. On the far bank a field of hay drying in the sun exhaled the heady fragrance of summer.

Several more pools proved no easier than the first and at length I admitted defeat, decided I should try another day and walked back to my vehicle. After a cup of tea I set off for home, drove along the valley and in passing the next farm, Oareford, met Jono Woollacott. Getting down from his tractor at the roadside, he told me he had been cutting grass for silage and made some progress but had several more acres to cut. It is impossible not to like this hard working farmer with a whole-some face. I told him I had been fishing on Mike and Molly's water but admitted my lack of success.

"I used to love fishing! I went fishing every day when I was a boy," he said. "I'd come home from school and get the rod out. Every day! Didn't use flies, I used worms. I used to catch trout to give my mother to cook until I think she got tired of them."

His tattersall check shirt and jeans dusty with pollen, Jono leaned against the massive hind wheel of his tractor and I asked how old he was when he started fishing.

"Oh, little. When I first started fishing I was too small to be allowed a real hook. I was given a little ball of plasticine on the end of the line and had no idea why I didn't catch fish."

With a wry smile, he went on.

"One day there was a chap here who used to come and stay for the pony fair. He put a frozen salmon on my line and pretended I had caught it. And I imagined I had! They all had such a laugh. Then I finally got proper hooks and learned to use worms."

"What sort of worms?" I was entranced by these reminiscences and wanted to encourage more.

"Oh, any sort. I'd dig them up or find one under a stone. It had to be a little worm, just big enough to cover the hook. I used to think that a bigger worm would catch a bigger fish, and it might, but usually the fish just nibble at the ends of the worm without taking the hook. Smaller hooks and smaller worms are definitely better."

Wade was perfectly content to change between fishing with flies and worms as conditions dictated and had written of worm fishing, 'Don't you believe that it is quite an inferior kind of sport and hardly to be named amongst fly fishermen. This is all utter nonsense.' But I knew little about it so was interested to hear, and as he warmed to his subject Jono's face shone with enthusiasm.

"Sometimes I got the hook too deeply embedded in the worm, so the whole of the hook was covered, and then the fish would swallow the worm with the hook inside and instead of catching in its mouth it would go down into its belly and I couldn't get it out."

A strong athletic looking sheepdog, black and white and tan, came to sit at Jono's feet, leaning against his legs, gazing upwards adoringly.

"Hello Bruce," Jono said, ruffing his ears; and Bruce listened to the tales as he went on.

"One day I caught a very little fish, it was too small to keep so I threw it back and as it went I saw a really big fish dart out and grab it. I think it was a big old cannibal trout. So, of course, I tried to catch that fish but I never did. Those cannibal trout come out at night. I put a little fish on a hook and fxed up my rod so I could leave it there all night. In the morning the bait fish had been bitten about but it hadn't caught anything. I used to go out at night with a light and sometimes I saw huge fish in the water. Sometimes there were salmon, but I never see salmon up this far now. People tell me they don't get above Brendon."

Luttrell recorded fish of up to four pounds caught on night lines in some of the deep pools of Oare Water and Wade had written that the highest point on the river he caught salmon was just below Malmsmead, a couple of miles above Brendon and downstream of Oareford. So the tradition of hauling big fish out of this small stream was well established. This farm on the banks of Oare Water was a wonderful place for an enterprising boy to grow up; what exciting escapades he must have had designing his own fish-catching ruses which sometimes, triumphantly, succeeded. How could the thrill of the stream not be washed indelibly into his bones?

"I was apprehended by the Water Bailiff when I was nine," Jono announced. "I was fishing just where the stream goes through our yard but he told me off and sent me home because the season had finished."

"In your own yard?" I sympathised.

"Yes," he said, without apparently appreciating the irony, but stood taller and drew his shoulders back a little as he claimed, "I was the youngest person he had ever caught!"

CHAPTER 10

Chalk Water

———

Chalk Water runs through one of the wildest, loveliest valleys of Exmoor and in fishing it I hoped that Mr Wade should be my guide as he wrote with generous detail about fishing this stream, so I planned to take him with me and follow his advice as much as I could. It was a sunny July day with a light westerly breeze and, whilst the nicest sort of weather to be out on the moor, perhaps rather brighter than would be ideal for fishing in a stream with little shade. However, I was encouraged by Wade's opinion that Chalk Water is one where you should choose your stream according to the wind. The most perfect weather, he assures us, is with an upstream breeze, just enough to make a nice ripple on the still water. Warm weather is best, with fleeting clouds, and a light shower or two does no harm. So even though the water was rather low and clear, the weather was almost perfect.

Wade tells us that Chalk Water was about the best stream on Exmoor for its number of fish and ease of fishability. It had been called the Ladies' Stream, and he remembered a sportswoman who used to ride out on her pony from Porlock to fish here, knowingly choosing her day, and sometimes securing three to four score of trout. I wonder who she was and imagine a small wiry figure with pert eyes dapping along at a smart trot on an Exmoor pony – what a marvellous character she must have been.

As the day was so warm I did not bother with waders but wore leaky old walking boots which, if no longer efficient at keeping water out at least do not keep it in, and decided to take my old wicker creel. I had no intention of even attempting to fill it with fish as Wade would have done, but it was light and spacious and made a suitable container for my lunch, notebook and smallest binoculars, and if it got really hot it could also take my waistcoat. But it seldom gets really hot on Exmoor .

Wade explains how it was only necessary to call at the cottage of the old keeper, Joe Kingdom of Oareford, and pay him the sum of one shilling to procure a day's fishing here. Though Joe Kingdom has long gone I did start at Oareford, parking under a shady beech, and walked up the road to the little pool at the junction of Chalk Water and Weir Water, and a short way above there into the gated track between two walls on the right, just as Wade describes. I shouldn't think this lane has changed much since he walked it; the walls are probably medieval and a hundred years or so would make little difference to them. I expect magenta foxgloves, pink stonecrop and blue sheepsbit flowered on them then, just as they do now.

After passing a couple of small, enclosed meadows the path leads onto the moor and to the edge of the stream. 'Here, down under the wall put your rod and tackle together,' Wade advises, but I had already done that. Swallows swooped over the stream, looping their metallic glittering chains of song through the air, a family of hedge sparrows squabbled amiably in the hedge on the far bank and a green woodpecker laughed at me from an ash tree. He was probably right.

Wade's idea for having a small spike at the butt of your rod was interesting. He explains that without it the rod will occasionally have to be laid down amongst bracken and heather causing entanglement and delay. This sounded like a useful gadget but I did not have one so should have to manage without, though entanglement and delay would be inevitable sooner or later.

Wade then goes on to talk about his gut collar which, having been kept around the crown of his hat, must be seen to run straight and evenly and must be soaked for a while before beginning to fish. This seems like rather a performance and, despite my dislike of much about the modern world, I am grateful for tapered nylon leaders and fine monofilament tippets which are largely maintenance free and need no such nursing to work effectively.

I headed upstream where sheep grazed between clumps of gorse and on the way frequent little pools looked too inviting to pass by without casting a fly. Mr Wade warns, 'let your chief thought be to conceal yourself from the trout you are fishing for,' and I did all I could to make use of available cover. 'This lower part of Chalk is quite good water with small pools and runs, and the banks are a little humpy, so there is plenty of scope for manoeuvring,' he tells us, and clambering about I tried to conceal myself amongst the convenient humps, tall grasses and rocks along the edge of the stream, just as he said.

'Throw your Red Ant and Water Cricket gently at the lowest part' of a pool, Wade instructs, 'first by letting it out from where you stand, then by steadily and stoopingly creeping along the bank.' Well, that's what I tried to do, though I used only one fly at a time as I find, except in the most straightforward conditions with no bushes and no breeze, that two can lead to a tangle.

Wade assured me I should get many rises as I went along but in the first two or three pools I did not get one. There were fish there. I could see them. Especially when, having been shown my fly and discourteously ignoring it, they were alarmed by the line when I made the next cast. I began to revise my concern for the water and its numbers of fish and my respect for Mr Wade and the sportswoman from Porlock increased as I recognised they must have been very skilful fishermen indeed.

I tried a Red Ant which I had studiously tied on a number fourteen hook but lost it in a withy bush so replaced it with a Black Ant but that proved impossible to see on the water however squintingly I peered. Puzzling over my fly tin I found a brown fly with a chestnut hackle and knotted pheasant-tail filament legs that looked not unlike a small daddy long legs or the water crickets I could see skating about in the margins. The fish were unimpressed. So I resorted to one of my favourites, an Adams with a pale orange post to help me keep it in view.

Following Wade's directions for stoopingly, creepingly inching along the bank and casting a little further each time, I tried to disturb no fish except the one I hoped might be tempted to accept my fly. I came to a little rocky place where a few ash trees stand over the water and a line of tall beeches on an old hedge-bank is set back from the opposite bank. Stealthily, sneakingly I sat amongst bracken to cast up towards the top of the pool and watched my fly bob merrily back on the current. Halfway down the pool the fly was swallowed and a beautiful little Exmoor trout made my acquaintance. He was silver and gold, spotted with ruby, bright as a jewel and lively as the little green grasshopper who came jumping onto my hand to see. We both admired him for a moment before I let him speed away back into the current.

Satisfied enough to pause, I sat on the bank to take a sip of cool stream water and to eat my lunch of apple, celery and cheese. A wren sang from a thorn bush and, far down the valley, a half grown lamb demanded its mother.

It was not long before I set off again steadily, skulkingly stealing along the bank, lurking in the bracken and casting where I could. I passed a little meadow where the air was loud with an industry of bees from a line of hives just inside the stone-faced hedgebank and thought how delicious honey would be from this wild valley.

Above the meadow the stream's course is all through open moorland on both sides. Close to the bottom of Blindwell

Combe a fledgeling wren landed on a bracken frond beside me. His juvenile plumage was soft mottled brown, underwings speckled as a thrush, his short stubby tail erect. He watched me with great interest whilst his panicking mother fussed and scolded from the opposite bank but he was quite unafraid – just curious.

After a little distance I caught another trout, darker than the first, with a chocolate brown back and rich butter yellow belly with smaller black spots and tiniest dots of red. I returned him squiggling free to become once again part of the bubbling energy of the welcoming current.

I worked my way up the water, stoopingly, creepingly trying to cast whilst sitting or kneeling and tearing my trousers while lurkingly, crouchingly trying to avoid detection. Keeping low in the bracken avoided casting shadows or reflections over the water but had other disadvantages as my line sometimes became entangled in the fronds, but that risk seemed to be justified as I got a few rises although was frequently too slow to connect. And I learned that, at a distance, even a perfectly executed cast is ineffective if there is too much line on the water for a quick strike. I also learned that bracken and hemlock water dropwort are the two most snaggling plants in the world. Only let your line lightly touch the harshly toothed fronds and it is snatched instantly and grasped irretrievably, as though the plants suspected your motives and sought to protect their stream's fish. Perhaps they do.

So I sat still for a little while and ate some chocolate which I was pleased to discover in a pocket of my waistcoat and which was not quite melted. The air smelled of sheep and crushed bracken. Bell heather was beginning to flower in deep magenta drops and where it found sanctuary from the teeth of nibbling sheep and deer, safe within a thorn bush, it stood higher than my head, filling the bush with colour. A stonechat chinked from the topmost twig of a thorn and wind whispered over brackeny hills swelling upwards on either hand to meet the mares-tail swept heavens.

As I moved creepingly, stoopingly upstream the water became darker with peat stain until it was the colour of black tea. The sun was dropping towards the beetling brow of Stowey Allotment and, although there would be at least two hours before dark, yet in the stiffening breeze I became concerned that when the sun fell so would the temperature. I was wet and did not have a pullover.

"Just one more pool," I kept thinking; but then the next one looked even more inviting and so the chuckling stream enticed me along.

I reached the junction pool where a little stream comes down Outer Alscott Combe from Mill Hill to join the Chalk. Rugged slabs of rock appeared thrown down across the stream though were more likely heaved up out of the earth, waterworn edges rounded and knubbled, fissures softened with moss, dividing a series of pools linked by little tumbling waterfalls.

Deep moss scattered brightly with the delicate bells of pink bog pimpernel and sky blue ivy-leaved bellflower made a soft pillow to kneel on; it soaked through my thin trousers but kindly cushioned my bony knees. The pool just above was almost black, flecked with scraps of foam at its head where white water tumbled in. My rod had to be kept high on the back cast to avoid thorns behind, as I aimed my fly for the head of the pool where it landed on the edge of the bubbles. Almost at once the fly was engulfed by an electrified body, leaping and splashing on the end of my line. This was a larger fish and he took longer to draw in. When I brought him to hand he was breathtakingly handsome, dark olive bronze above and coppery gold below, darkly spotted in the colour of the peat soil, his lateral line finely dotted with scarlet. I laid him in the grass to admire him. This fish, I thought, might come home for supper.

Wade always fished with the aim of filling his creel and procuring food; it never occurred to him not to kill fish unless they were very undersized indeed (three and a half inches was suggested as a suitable limit) and out of every hundred fish he caught he reckoned to return just fifteen to seventeen. Today, being mindful of wild fish populations, catch and release has become a usual practice almost everywhere other than on stocked waters. If every angler killed every fish he caught there would certainly be a detrimental impact on numbers, yet I firmly believe the strongest influence is from habitat quality and food abundance. Though compelled by an irresistible desire to more fully connect with the valley, even taking this one fish was not done without some sense of guilt. Yet, so many times I have returned fresh rod-caught trout to the stream only to open a tin of smaller and much staler sardines for supper (I would never buy farmed salmon) and wondered whether buying into an industrial scale fishing operation is not worse. I'm unsure, but I do not often kill fish.

A sense of place is felt most profoundly when that place is experienced through all the senses. Having gazed in awe upon this landscape, felt its wind and sun on my skin, the quickness of fishy life in my fingers, listened to birdsong and streamsong and tasted its water, I felt I carried within myself a little of the essence of the valley, sharing in its physical being as well as holding the memory of its presence in my heart. A supper of Chalk Water trout would both physically and spiritually consummate that eucharistic connection with this ancient land.

I wrapped the trout in bracken fronds, placed him reverently in my airy creel where he would stay cool and turned reluctantly for home. As I went I thanked whatever gods there may be in the valley for the day and the stream and the fish and ahead of me a lithe russet form with white tagged brush turned his head towards me, nodding briefly, as he trotted across my path.

CHAPTER 11

Chocolate is the New Smoking

"I used to fish all this water when I was a kid," said Chris as we drove over Robber's Bridge. All the way along the valley he claimed, "I've had some trout out of here," at every pool we passed. When we reached the broad grassy area at Oareford he told me he used to camp there and waved an arm towards the beeches standing over the stream. "There was a good pool in those trees – we called it the grasshopper pool because we used to catch grasshoppers for bait – they were brilliant. Or worms." Chris's childhood memories of Weir Water, Oare Water and Chalk Water were rekindled by the streams, reawakening his childlike sense of fun so it was like fishing with a six foot two little boy.

It was a day of hot blue sky broken with black clouds glowering in from the sea on the west wind. Chalk Water was lowish, though not as low as last time I was here, and the colour of weak black tea. We could see fish and they could see us; they were very wild and very, very spooky.

I had never known Chris find it so difficult to catch a fish, although the grin never left his face. In the first pool he had three rises but no fish. In the second, two rises and got hung up in a bramble. In the third pool, at last, he had one and that brought us both a genuine smile but, goodness, they were tricky. I had a few casts through the next couple of pools with no result. Taking turns to fish and to watch, we progressed slowly up the water. The fishing was hard.

Claude Wade, of fishing this very stretch, had written, 'So you go along under the best conditions of wind and water, and in one of these long reaches, running from two to three feet deep, for a length of about fifteen yards, you may, as I have done, catch six or eight trout by careful fishing.'

How did he do that? How *did* he do it? We fished the same water and there seemed to be little difference in our approach. Could the challenges of fishing low water be a recent phenomenon? It seems unlikely as there have always been variations in rainfall and water conditions and the driest year on record was 1855. Could Wade's nine foot six greenheart rod be more effective than our six or seven feet of carbon, or his gut casts that needed soaking before he started fishing? Tackle has only changed because the newer ideas are more efficient; if they hadn't worked they would never have sold and production would quickly have ceased. We can only trust that modern tackle gives us advantage over the old. There is no doubt Wade was a good fisherman – he had fished these streams for forty years although, as a visitor, he admits to being handicapped by seldom being able to take his fishing before August and September. Chris must have considerably more local fishing experience and I know him to be a piscatorial genius. My primary reason for bringing him along that day was to make certain that my modest catch rates were due to more than inexperience and poor performance, yet even he was unable to approach Wade's phenomenal rate of success.

Often exceeding a century, Wade wrote, 'about ten dozen has been rather a favourite number with me, but only once have I exceeded a hundred and twenty-five, and that was on a good day up Chalk and the head of Badgworthy (walking from one to the other over the hills) when, fishing from 9 a.m. to 5 p.m., I got one hundred and sixty-seven.' That meant catching over twenty fish an hour, or one every three minutes. How, I wondered, could we ever hope to compete with that? Chris seldom fishes for such long days, preferring to fit in a couple of hours here and there several times a week, but I wanted to know how many fish he thought he could catch in a day if he really tried.

"I dare say, if I set my mind to it, I could go all out and catch thirty or forty."

"Could you catch 120? On a really good day?"

"No. No way."

I related Wade's estimate of catching six to eight from each run of around fifteen yards and his advice to always draw a hooked fish firmly downwards to avoid disturbing the others up above. Chris was incredulous. "There must have been so many fish here then. Hundreds!"

Other stories of long-ago fishing here were recorded by Claude Luttrell who frequently travelled from his home at Dunster to stay with his friend and mentor, Mr Snow, a first rate fisherman whose land included Oare Water, Badgworthy, Weir and Chalk. Luttrell took great pleasure in these varied waters in wild country where, though he seldom fished all day, he remembers how on a good fishing day you could soon fill your basket with small, delicious trout.

One of his tales is particularly interesting. He tells us that Snow 'couldn't beat the record of Parson Froude, who caught 315 trout in one day!' Parson Froude was a notorious rogue with scant regard for the truth and even any corroboration of witnesses was likely to have been obtained under duress, so if Luttrell really meant what he wrote I am unconvinced of its accuracy. I wonder whether Luttrell made a mistake here, though, and was really referring to Parson Gould, in whose achievement we may have some confidence as both Wade and Thornton wrote of him catching over 300 in a day. Anyway, whatever the truth of that record of 315, Mr Snow set out to beat it. Luttrell tells us 'He started off at 5.30 one morning in June, with his man carrying a second rod, so that no time would be wasted if a fly got hitched or a fish broke the cast. He filled several baskets, but had to admit himself defeated with a total catch of 265!'

We are not told how long Mr Snow fished that day, though being June it could have been a long day. He must have paused occasionally to take refreshment and to travel between different streams, which he might have done on a pony but more likely on foot; either way, it isn't far but it is steep. Supposing he actually fished for twelve hours – that would mean he caught just over twenty two fish an hour. You couldn't do it today, even with a man to carry a second rod and a groom to bring a horse.

The inescapable conclusion, Chris and I both agreed, was that the fish population must have reduced dramatically from what it had been a century ago. We could see no obvious reason for this; the stream and its moorland setting appear unchanged yet must, in some obscure way, be profoundly damaged.

A wagtail bounced along the stream and a red kite sailed over the valley, massive wingspan stretched wide to catch the breeze, tail forked like a fish's, wheeling the thermal. Creeping forward to sit low on the bank I cast into a little pool where the stream swirled in from the right, and a ewe watched me intently from the opposite bank. I sent the back cast over my left shoulder to avoid an ash tree behind me, and aimed my fly into the fast water first, where ripples might obscure the leader; then to the right where a mossy rock sheltered a pocket of still water behind it, just the sort of place a fish might loiter; then a slightly longer cast to stretch across the main current into an eddy where bubbles rotated on water turning back from the main flow into a bowl scooped in the rock around it. The fly was received with a splashy rise, I flicked up the rod and felt fish. For an instant. But then he was gone and the fly came back bedraggled and rejected. The ewe was still watching, apparently captivated by my mysterious performance. Goodness knows what she thought of it.

Wade referred to his favourite fishing flies as his 'pet flies', those in which he had most confidence and which caught him most trout. Accepting his knowledge and experience in this matter, I was keen to try the same ones. The Red Ant, he said, was his best friend and the fishes' greatest enemy during August and September. I had made a very simple version from russet floss bound around the hook shank in two knobs with a narrow waist between, forming the shape of an ant body with a red cock hackle in front to imitate legs and lift the little fly up on the water. It had already proved effective.

Next, Wade recommended a Water Cricket which, he writes, is meant to imitate the spiders seen darting about greasily on the top of the water, and described the dressing as a yellow body with a twist of black silk around it and a black hackle. Water crickets are not really spiders but bugs similar to water measurers and pond skaters, though shorter and stouter than either with disturbingly fast spidery movement. I had often seen them in pockets of slow water under the banks, although I had never seen a trout take one. Nevertheless, I followed Wade's recipe to the letter and made a few.

Another of Wade's favourites, especially for hot weather, was a Governor. It took a little searching to find the dressing for this fly, which must once have been sufficiently common for Wade to think it unnecessary to describe, but has now fallen so far out of fashion no one seems to have heard of it. I eventually discovered a recipe as follows: a few fibres of red cock's hackle for a tail, a body with two turns of yellow floss, the remainder of peacock herl, a red hackle and wings of hen pheasant or woodcock. So I made some of those too, and had a selection of all three in my fly tin.

There were large sedge flies on the water but fish would not rise to Chris's Deer Hair Sedge, nor to his long-tailed small Adams that always works. I rose a fish to a Water Cricket and another to a Governor but missed them both before eventually catching a lively little trout, dark backed and bright bellied, his energetic splashes sparkling in the sun. Chris was satisfactorily impressed.

"What did you catch that on?"

"A Red Ant."

"Have you got any more?"

"Yes, plenty." (I refrained from adding, 'thanks'.)

Chris looked quite wounded as he demanded, "Hand one over!"

As we continued upstream Chris caught a few more fish, I missed a few more. We reached a pool with grassy banks like a sheep nibbled lawn amid the bracken and I sat on the right bank with a few clumps of rushes for cover, shuffled quietly into position and then made Chris wait before I would cast, rummaging in my waistcoat pocket.

"I need some chocolate."

Chris laughed. "It used to be called a cigarette!"

Yes – Arthur Applin often paused to light a pipe, Henry Williamson always carried one and I had heard various people say that giving up smoking inhibited their ability to catch fish. I think I understand why; it's not the tobacco, although perhaps the calming influence of nicotine may help, but I believe simply stopping and watching the water is productive. Being still for a while is certainly useful because fish see movement. Most helpful of all though is becoming centred in the moment, gathering our rambling thoughts so prone to dragging back to past memories or galloping off to future plans to focus on the now of the present, just as the river between upstream and downstream pauses here at this pool not stopping exactly but slowing to take a proper look, so we should pause in our haste to allow the moment to catch up with us, taking a deep breath, taking time, taking the moment and holding it in our hands, turning it this way and that, examining it closely in every detail, allowing awareness to bloom until it spreads over the moment like a drop of oil dripped on the pool before us. Only when this heightened level of consciousness is reached are we in the optimum place to cast for a fish; to cast as if it were the only task in the world to perform; as if it were the last cast we would ever make. In this state of being it might possibly work not by lucky chance as it may sometimes work at other times but with a calm sureness, not necessarily seeing fish feeding yet choosing the right fly and knowing where to put it and knowing when it will be taken and, through knowing, being ready.

So when I had eaten a piece of chocolate (my favourite dark chocolate with sea salt) I cast into the pool, working the fly up the water in three stages and when it reached the side of the bubbles coming into the head of the pool it was taken and I lifted the rod to feel a good sized fish. He zipped down the pool like a bullet but soon came to hand and he was truly stunning – about ten inches, a bronzy green with a brassy yellow belly and, unusually, with no black spots at all. Those spots he had were few but large and were of a foxy russet red set within chalky haloes.

"Oh, nice fish!" Chris enthused, pulling his phone out of his waistcoat. "That's the biggest one of the day." I wanted him to take a picture of the trout but he kept photographing me instead, and I must have had an immodestly huge grin.

"The chocolate worked," I said.

"Yes – chocolate is the new smoking."

As we walked back downstream towards the road we looked up at hills bright with emerald bracken and magenta bell heather, the sky boiling with heavy cloud, and just as we reached the car at Oareford it began to rain; soft fat drops releasing a deep chord of scent, rich and spicy as fruit cake, steaming from the warm earth.

CHAPTER 12

Weir Water

———

The wild majesty of the Weir Water valley lies, in its lower reaches, between woodland and pasture on one side and heather moorland of Mill Hill on the other. Its upper part, on Porlock Allotment, is entirely moorland stretching almost to Lucott Cross where the little stream arises on the narrow watershed between tributaries of the River Lyn and Horner Water.

Ian Baldock is the Estate Manager for Lillycombe Sporting Club and we met as arranged on the road below Oare Post. Ian was enthusiastically welcoming and tirelessly voluble.

"It's great to meet you!" he said, getting out of his pick-up truck and coming across to shake hands. "You're very welcome here, we love it when someone takes a genuine interest in the place. Come any time you like."

"Thank you *so* much, it's such a fantastic place."

"We love it here, and we are doing everything possible to improve it for wildlife. Though we have possibly got too many deer."

Ian told me about the estate – pheasants, partridges and game crops, whilst a liver and white spaniel peered from the back of his truck. It was clear he was passionate about making conservation work alongside the shooting business.

"I hope you'll find the stream is in good condition – we never use any chemical sprays or fertilisers anywhere near it. We were quite shocked when someone found lots of dead frogs and accused us of polluting the water."

"Dead frogs?"

"Well, frog and toad skins."

"What time of year was that?" I asked.

"January."

Standing in the narrow road we talked about how otters gorge on frogs and toads when they come out to start spawning in January and February.

"They do seem to spit the skins out," I said. "I bet that was otters. They live on all the Exmoor streams; although you don't often see them it's easy to find signs they've been there."

The evidence pointed to otters as the most likely culprits and Ian seemed relieved that there may be a natural explanation.

"Right, let's go." Ian led the way down a track descending into a steep sided valley to a meadowy spot close to the water where rocky mounds set with mature ash, sycamore and oak gave shelter and seclusion to the glade they enclosed.

"What an idyllic spot," I said, getting out of my vehicle. "This is so lovely, thank you. I can walk down to the bottom of the valley, fish up to here and stop for lunch and then go on upstream for the afternoon. It's perfect!"

"You enjoy yourself. I've got to get back to my birds, we released a new batch at five o'clock this morning," Ian said. Swinging his truck around, he leaned through the window and called goodbye. "Hope you have a good day. Let me know how you get on."

Ian left me to the peace of this untroubled valley and as his vehicle receded up the dusty track the presence of the land surged back to fully occupy the quiet space. The deep valley is enclosed by precipitous hills clad on one side with oak woodland and, on the other, with heather and fresh young bracken just overgrowing the dead tan litter of last year's growth. It was astonishing to think that the little stream tinkling along the bottom must have carved this dramatic landscape, digging a home for itself as industriously as a mole or a badger.

The water was clear and low with wind from the west or north west, bowling blowsy grey cumulous in from the sea, somewhat stronger than would have been ideal but at least it was blowing upstream. I wandered the banks through grassy meadows starry with constellations of pignut and bedstraw flowers and wet flushes colourful with ragged robin and forget-me-not. The luxury of leaving lunch with my vehicle in the middle of the beat meant I had very little to carry. When I came within sight of the road at Robber's Bridge I turned around to fish back upstream.

At a nice little pool below an ash tree I knelt in the bracken and watched the water. Making time for observation is important and I know I can be too hasty sometimes. So I felt the coolness of the water and surprising warmth of the wet grass on the bank and tried to see what insects were about. Although unable to name many of them, trying to use an artificial fly that looks similar to the live insects on the stream seems a reasoned approach. There was not a huge number that morning but a wide variety.

I selected a small mayfly pattern with a ribbed white body, blue grey hackle and a long tail. The pool was not very large, there seemed little point working up it in stages so I simply cast towards the water tumbling in at the head, under the ash tree. The fly fell onto the sun shattered, rock ruffled surface and was lost to sight amongst reflections and ripples. Where was it?

Gloop! Ah, there it was – too late. Although I berated myself for missing the strike I was encouraged by the hefty splosh of the rise; it seemed like a good sized fish for a small pool in a small stream, and my choice of fly had been accepted with enthusiasm.

Wade tells us that on Weir Water he found fish a trifle larger, or at least longer, than on Chalk, but not quite so plentiful. He writes of a particular scarcity above Weir Wood which he puts down to 'wormers' and 'gropers' coming down across the Porlock and Exford road, explaining that poaching was encouraged

by crowds of visitors at hotels and lodging houses wanting trout for their breakfasts. No doubt poaching was also driven by a genuine need to put food on Victorian family tables. I don't think poaching wild trout on a commercial scale happens much on Exmoor these days perhaps partly because, with the easy availability of rifles, serious poachers have moved on to larger prey.

The next pool was longer so I made a series of casts, working forward a couple of feet at a time towards the oak tree at its head. On the third cast my fly rose a fish but I missed the strike again for the same reason – amongst the ditsy of white bubbles and hawthorn petals on the water I couldn't see the fly.

A cheery wren came down the stream, hopping from stone to stone, and clung daintily to a bramble hanging over the water from the bank beside me. It was so close I instinctively froze to watch the little bird. The tiniest creature, no bigger than a pheasant's egg, yet wren-song is enormous; piercing and far reaching it usually dominates the chorus of birds in a hedge.

The wren flew back upstream and I made the next cast towards the top of the pool. It was taken again. I missed it again. I gave up on that fly. And on the pool. The wren had returned and was looking towards her dangling bramble but seemed reluctant to pass me. Probably, I thought, she had a nest there, so I moved away.

The mayfly had been good, the fish had liked it but, through no fault of its own, was not working because I couldn't see it. So I put on a reddish fly chosen for its bushy orange post. I wasn't sure what the fish would make of it but the orange post was unmissable.

At the first cast this fly was taken into the twigs of an ash by a gust of wind and I stood over the pool to retrieve it. The dead ash twigs snapped easily and I rescued the fly but abandoned the pool as any fish in it must have seen my teetering and stretching acrobatics and I wondered whether it was worth it for this peculiarly clumsy looking fly. Wade sensibly reminds us that if the arms and head of the fisherman appear on top of the bank against the sky, he would do no more harm to his chances of catching fish if he were to throw half a brick into the pool below him.

There was one more pool before the car and lunch and I crawled up to it between half grown bracken fronds and tall horse thistles to sit on a clump of heather. Water swirled between rocks of grey and beige, some splodged with black algae, some furred with moss, and cast towards bubbles tumbling into the top of the pool. I could see the fly clearly but would the fish like it?

Yes!

This fish did like it, the hook connected and a golden flank flashed as he cartwheeled around the sunlit pool on my quivering line. Soon he came to hand; a black and scarlet spotted fish with a brassy sheen and a belly the colour of the tormentil and birds-foot-trefoil flowering on the bank. And I learned that the appearance of a fly to the fisherman is as important as its appearance to the fish. The trout shimmered back to the laughing current putting a smile on my face just in time for lunch and I realised how hungry I was.

That splendid, sun-warmed valley was a perfect place to enjoy my picnic of cheese and apple and, had I known it wouldn't have to be carried, I should have brought more. Wade, writing of this excellent little stream, says that, even if you have an indifferent day as far as fish go, you have real typical Exmoor scenery to enjoy, and I had to agree; it was a truly lovely place and cannot have altered much since he was here some hundred and twenty years ago or more. But whilst appreciating the landscape there was little time to dawdle, a quick cup of tea and piece of flapjack and I was off again.

The first pool of the afternoon looked enticingly wide open and easy to cast into yet as I planned my approach I heard voices and, looking back down the valley, saw a group of people with children and dogs splashing about in the stream. They were heading this way.

Perhaps if I'm quick, I thought, I could have a few casts and be done before they get here. I waded out across the tail of the pool but in my hurry was careless and slipped on the greasy stones, making almost as much noise as the children and dogs. I cast the fly up the pool a few times, looking back over my shoulder between each one with all the wariness of a poacher. If fish saw my fly, they ignored it. More likely they had vacated the pool at the first sound of me scummering about on the stones. As I said, I am frequently too hasty.

There was plenty of fresh water ahead of me so leaving that pool behind I marched on briskly hoping to get well ahead of the ramblers. When I reached a wooden footbridge the way ahead was overhung with thorns, the path melted into rushes and squelchy ground. I thought it unlikely that a family enjoy-ing an afternoon stroll would venture far into that sort of country and did not see them again.

A little further along there was a pool whose smooth, clear water was watched over by a hawthorn from the right bank and a mossy-trunked ash tree from the left, with roots leaning along the bank like folded arms. Ferns fringed the unfathomable depths like the lashes of downcast eyes. I could see fish moving there so perhaps they could see me. Perhaps it was too clear, too still. But perhaps I would try.

I crossed to the right bank well below the pool, crept up to it, sat on a stone at the foot of the bank and watched. There were two decent fish below the ash roots but a small fish close to the tail of the pool was no more than a few feet away and I could see parr markings smudging his flank. There was no way to cast without him seeing me move and he would alert all the others. I ate chocolate. There were plenty of fish rising further up the pool and after a while the parr left his position so I decided to try a cast.

With my first back cast the fly caught in a hawthorn bush and attempting to flick it out broke the tippet. So I left it there and selected another. This time a little grey fly with a small orange post and two whisks for a tail. Sometimes the fly snagged in bracken or river-stone moss but I kept shuffling furtively along the bank, staying low and sitting on stones, turf, clumps of rushes, pushing backwards into a hollow place to allow slightly more space in front of me for a side cast to unfold. Sometimes the fly drifted amongst bubbles and hawthorn petals on the dark water under the ash, sometimes it hesitated as it touched a bramble hanging into the stream from the left. A couple of times the fly came close to fish. Fish looked at it. They refused. They were not spooked though so I stayed still and tried a small, yellow bodied spent mayfly pattern with splayed white wings. This was also declined. Yet still fish were rising. It was hard to see what they were taking, but it looked small so I tried a tiny black gnat, rolled it gently onto the water and it was accepted with a cheerful splip!

A bright little fish came in on my line, gold as sunlight on the pebbly stream bed and silver as sunlight on the shimmering surface. When I released him he zoomed back to his friends in the pool and I felt sure his obvious shock and distress would spread alarm, so I sat still and ate more chocolate and fish continued to rise.

The little fly was dried and plumped up between my fingers and then cast forward again on another quest. It landed to the left, near the bramble, twired around a bit and then started to drag so I lifted it off and tried again. This time it drifted slowly past the ash roots, past the spot where the two fish had been holding station together, and kept moving, ignored. At the next cast the little fly fell in the centre of the stream, near the head of the pool, where there was a little surface movement and the tippet was lost amongst fine ripples and as it drifted back into the centre of the pool it was taken by another pretty little fish who came to hand and whose freedom was soon restored.

Fish continued to rise and I felt then that I could have sat there for hours and might have pulled fish after fish from the pool but the sun was lost in dark cloud, the breeze was strengthening, the temperature falling and I was getting stiff. It was time to move.

I retrieved the fly lost earlier in the hawthorn bush and, despite having decided I had finished fishing, attached it to my line before following a deer path back down the valley. Close to the wooden footbridge I paused to watch a family of young bluetits who had just fledged and were all shouting for mother; a dipper dropped from under the bridge and arrowed away upstream; a moth lay on the path, big wings patterned like oak bark. And although it was delightful there I was glad I had only to walk as far as the little meadow where my vehicle waited with a cup of tea and not all the way to Lynmouth as Wade might have done.

To reach the crossing place it was necessary to walk past the big wide pool on a high bank close to the water's edge. Evening was drawing on, there were a few insects over the water and as I crossed the stream I thought I might as well try a cast. Any fish would already have seen me above the water on the high path so there was little hope but, well . . .

So, standing halfway across the tail I cast up the pool and a little fish was spooked and darted past me downstream. It was late and I was tired so I wasn't being very careful and though there was no cover at all I walked up the shillets on the left bank to reach the faster water at the top of the pool. My fly was drowned in the turbulence. I dried it off and tried again.

Nothing. I would have one last cast and finish.

Nothing.

Just one more then.

And finally he came, devouring the fly in an enormous gulp; I lifted into a weighty tug and as he roared around the pool, bending my little rod and leaping clear of the water three times, I realised this was a substantial fish. He took a little longer to subdue but eventually came to my net and what a magnificent trout he was; a solid nine and a half inches of gleaming bronze splendour aflame in the lowering sun – royalty of the moorland stream.

CHAPTER 13

The East Lyn

White water charges down a chasm where precipitous woodland slips away to expose walls of raw rock, the river bed strewn
with boulders the size of cars. The name Lyn is derived from the
Anglo-Saxon 'Llynna', a torrent. Parts of the East Lyn's tumultuous course cannot be reached without ropes and crampons.
It feels forbiddingly unapproachable.

From the coastal town of Lynmouth to Watersmeet the winding road is busy with few spaces to park but I found a small
one and walked down a steep path to the bottom of the valley.
As I descended the air became progressively cooler through con-
toured layers of temperature, colder air sunk in the bowels of
the deep gorge seldom reached by sun and further chilled by icy
river water and the dank breath of the sea. The river was not
especially wide but ferociously powerful, progressing in a series
of waterfalls, deep pools and white rapids quite unlike the
moorland streams I was used to. I walked along the riverside
path and crossed at a wooden bridge with equal feelings of awe
and dismay.

The path on the right bank was crowded with tourists so I
returned to the left and found a couple of pools where water
widened out a little between rocks. At the head of the second
pool, which I worked out from the map must be Vellacott's

Pool, a handy rope hung from a tree to help scramble up a large rock. It was the only way to move upstream. My waders offered a poor grip on the sheer rock face, though with a lot of pulling arms, slithering feet and sore knees I eventually managed it. But further progress was effectively halted where a vertical cliff dropped into deep, fast water.

Wade loved the River Lyn and fished every pool of it for trout, salmon and peal, or sea trout, usually staying in one of the comfortable hotels in Lynton or Lynmouth. He warns us this part of the river is difficult to negotiate, that getting along the left bank is a nasty job with one spot about here tellingly called 'Bad Place', and recommends crossing over to the right bank above Vellacott's Pool, either by wading or by returning to the footbridge.

Vellacott's Pool was still very much as Wade described it with a dramatic waterfall plunging in at the head and foaming water swirling back across a wide pool to a shallow pebbly area offering sufficient space for a cast. But clearly my light seven-foot rod and dry fly were not going to be effective here. Trout in the little moorland streams I had fished lately were only a few ounces at best and my line was fitted with a three pound leader. Gazing at this powerful river I felt as if I had turned up at a business meeting dressed for a pyjama party.

At the bottom of a waistcoat pocket I found a tin of pathetically small nymphs and picked out a few with brass beads. I should need weight, I thought, to get down through the churning water. So I cast a few diminutive looking nymphs into the edges of the foam but it was clear they were not heavy enough; the tempestuous water tossed them back with contempt. It was like casting a line into a washing machine. How, I wondered, should I ever know if I had a bite?

Obviously, I caught nothing.

The capacity of a river to transmute from boisterous torrent to ferocious deluge of tsunamic proportions is breathtaking. On 15th of August 1952 the River Lyn did just that. After a wet fortnight the land of Exmoor was already saturated when nine inches of rain fell in twenty four hours, more than might usually be expected in three months concentrated into just one day. Water running off the moor was funnelled into this narrow gorge where constricting rock walls squeezed the spate into a deep channel like a water cannon of incredible velocity and aimed it at the town.

Heavy purple cloud obscured daylight so effectively that lights were lit at midday and it was quite dark by 5 o'clock. When daylight slowly returned the following morning it revealed a town largely destroyed. Shops and houses were demolished and streets buried twenty five feet deep in trees, mud and boulders weighing up to ten tons. The beach was covered with debris of timber and rubble, wreckage from smashed buildings, mangled cars and motorcycles, and a dead stag.

Every river and stream of the moor was affected, every valley-nestled village and farm suffered damage and people drowned on the Heddon and the Bray but at Lynmouth results were truly catastrophic. The flood took 132 vehicles, 93 buildings, 28 bridges and 34 human lives, 28 of them at Lynmouth and the nearby hamlet of Barbrook.

If Wade revisited the River Lyn today the greatest physical changes he might find would be those resulting from that one tragic night. Where it passes through the town, the East Lyn has been realigned, widened, deepened and contained within new walls to control any future insurrection. During the flood the West Lyn rose sixty feet above its normal level and realigned itself, returning to an earlier route it had once followed before being culverted through the town. Wade might not even recognise Lynmouth now.

At length I left the roaring current and walked back up the steep path to the road feeling quite ill equipped to fish such a river. I drove over Hillsford Bridge and up the hill onto Brendon Common where I stopped for a cup of tea, feeling a light wash of relief to be back on the moors. To the south, waves of moorland concealing those delightful little streams in their creases rolled out to the gently fading sky.

How could I ever fish such a violently torrential river as the Lyn, I wondered? The prospect seemed as hopeless as trying to reason with a large, drunken man in a temper whose language I could not speak. I decided I needed help.

* * *

Lewis Hendrie has fished the Lyn for seventeen years and I had heard tales of his prowess as a fisherman from his parents, Peter and Linda, who run The White Horse Hotel in Exford. They had told me how he grew up fishing in the River Exe outside their hotel and sometimes, when he was a small child, search parties had to be sent to find him as he blithely wandered along the river for hours.

It was a fine day but cold with a sharp wind when I met Lewis just outside Lynmouth. He rigged up our two ten foot rods, one with a nymph below a dry fly and another with two heavy nymphs, on long leaders with short lengths of fine yellow line between leader and tippet to act as indicators. Scraped with my fingernails (Lewis showed me how to do it but doesn't have fingernails himself) the yellow line sprang into coils which sat up on the water, making it easily visible without leaving much impression in the surface.

We began fishing at the bottom of the beat on the edge of Lynmouth and in the second pool Lewis caught a little trout, but said there were not as many there as he would usually find.

"Where do fish go in low water?" he wondered.

"Well, I suppose they find deep pockets and cool, shady spots and hide under ledges," I guessed.

"They must be still there. They're in the river somewhere, but you can't find them."

"No," I agreed. But argued, "You would think that if the river has half the usual volume of water, it must contain twice the usual density of fish. They should be easier to find." But we both knew they were not.

Lewis showed me how to, not cast exactly but lob the nymphs into a pool, swinging their weight around on the long leader using virtually no line. I was surprised by how close we could get to a pool without spooking the fish; turbulence shattered the surface window so we could not see into the water and the fish could not see out. However, the river was very low and clear and Lewis explained how these conditions made fishing more difficult than usual.

"In clear water you can't get close to fish in a still pool because they can see you coming. And if you're too far back it takes too long for your strike to be transmitted down the line." I knew there were times when I had missed fish for that reason, because my line was too long, but in clear water on small, shallow streams it was tricky to get close without good cover.

Lewis showed me his posh line snippers that cost £50, he said, and the manufacturing company would replace the blades for life, but I never saw him use them – he always cut line with his teeth.

We worked our way upstream, throwing two or three casts into each pool, holding most of the line off the water to avoid drag from the current and watching the coiled indicator. When the coils straighten, you strike, Lewis explained. Before long, I too pulled out a trout.

We scrambled around rocks, slithered down banks and generally scralled about, fishing each pool in the clear, deep parts just below white water. Lewis skipped over rocks, telling astonishing fishing tales and eating pasties as we went. I caught a few trout and a couple of salmon parr, both similarly darkly mottled and barred with parr smudges.

Lewis told me that ten years ago he would have caught at least twice the number of fish he could catch in the Lyn now, and they were much bigger too. When I asked him why he thought that might be, he was unsure but suggested that maybe intensifying agricultural practices had depleted the insects fish feed on. But I pointed out the whole valley is woodland for several miles, even the headwaters only pass through a few grass fields and above that is moorland. On farms along the whole length of this river and its tributaries grassland is managed with modest levels of fertiliser and there is no arable land. Most of the valley was ancient woodland and neither of us could understand what had changed so profoundly.

Watersmeet is where the East Lyn meets the hastening Combe Park Water, which is the lower end of Hoaroak Water, and the place is understandably popular with walkers who follow paths through woodland and along riverbanks. Compounding the attraction, the National Trust have a busy tea shop in the riverside house, but crowds are not conducive to fishing so Lewis and I decided to leave them behind, return to the road and drive further upstream to Rockford. There we found some lovely pools and a few more trout fell to our nymphs.

Then, just above Rockford Bridge we came to a section where the river dropped between high banks and we fished in green shade below a canopy of branches meeting overhead. And here, as I lifted the rod carelessly, my nymphs caught in overhanging ash twigs and would not tug free.

"Oh no, that's completely out of reach. I shall have to snap it off," I said, tightening the line.

"No, don't do that," Lewis said. "I can bend it down. Here, hold my rod."

The ash sprang from a cluster of coppice poles leaning out of the steep, mossy riverbank and Lewis clambered up towards them. I stood below the tree, holding our two rods in my left hand, stretching towards the nymphs with my right, waiting for him to press the branch down to within reach. Watching the dangling nymphs descend towards my waiting fingers, I didn't see Lewis climb out onto the trunk. Suddenly there was a sharp crack followed by a splintering crash and the whole tree came down on top of me in a tangle of torn leaves and shattered branches.

We both lived, and the rods appeared undamaged, but we never found the nymphs.

* * *

The garage at Barbrook sells tickets to fish the Watersmeet and Glenthorne Fisheries, which include most of the East Lyn River between Lynmouth and Brendon and there, the following week, I paid a reasonable £3.50 for a trout ticket and picked up a delicious homemade apple flapjack for my lunch. In 1902, when Mr Wade was writing his book, a day's fishing ticket cost two shillings and sixpence which, allowing for inflation, is the current equivalent of over £15.00, so we are very fortunate indeed that fishing here today is so accessible.

From the little parking place on the road above Lynmouth I walked down the steep path into the valley. Vellacott's Pool was deserted but the banks were wet and paw marks showed dogs had recently played in the water. Ah well, I thought optimistically, there are always so many people here, the fish must be used to them. It took a little while to set up my rod anyway so by the time I was ready the fish were rested and, I hoped, had time to recover from the paddling paws of rampaging dogs.

The new nymphs I had planned to make were going to be perfectly suited to these conditions, heavy with a hint of sparkle and a speck of colour. Tungsten beads for their heads had arrived in the post, but of course there hadn't been time for fly-tying, so instead I turned out all my old fly boxes and found a few that just might do.

The heaviest nymph I could find was tied on and I tried a few casts. I wasn't very good. The long leader was difficult to cast properly and this pool was bigger than those where Lewis's 'lobbing' method had been so effective. Several times the nymph snagged on rocks in the bottom. Nevertheless, I caught a beautiful little salmon parr in the shallow water at the foot of the swirling pool. Bright and lively as he wriggled away to freedom, he was a spark of hope in my relationship with this river.

Once favoured by poachers, Mr Wade wrote that during Victorian times Vellacott's Pool was more associated with illegal than legal fishing and describes how a dozen or more rods would haul out salmon by a variety of improper, foul and unfair means, more for the money to be made from the sale of fish than for sport. 'Vellacott's Pool became such a sink of iniquity that the humble legitimate fisherman was afraid to be seen there.'

He also says, 'It really is a splendid pool and has always struck me as being about the only one on the river where there is a clear cast for a salmon fly. A friend of mine tried it often with no success; in fact I don't believe a salmon has ever yet been caught fairly with the fly in the Lyn . . .' So perhaps my little parr, although small, was not an unworthy catch.

After a while the chill began to seep through my waders and, deciding I needed a walk, I set off down the riverbank path. Sun glowing on the wooded hilltops could not reach the bottom of the gorge but exercise warmed me up. Following a bit of a brisk walk I tried another spot which, from the map, I decided was Overflow Pool.

From the foot of the pool I worked my way forwards, creeping from rock to rock, throwing short casts ahead of me and watching coils of yellow indicator as I drew line back with the stream. I caught two little trout, small but delightful, and their splashy acceptance of my nymph felt like a heartening welcome from the river. The violent nature of its current and harsh features of its channel began to feel less hostile, less aloof, and with a growing recognition of the river's benign intent I felt I was, slowly, coming to understand a little of its language.

CHAPTER 14

Old Rods

—

Fishing the East Lyn became a regular thing and although on the furthest side of the moor from my home it is refreshing to make an occasional excursion there to experience the dramatic rock hewn gorge and its rapid river. However, I soon reverted to my favourite seven foot rod and a dry fly, sometimes changing to a nymph for the biggest pools, sometimes missing them out. Although it is the deepest darkest pools that give this river its unique character and forbidding quality, there are plenty of small pools and pockets between them where a dry fly seems to work well.

Rockford is a tiny village on a narrow road and my car had to squeeze tightly into the hedge to park where it would not be too much in the way. My plan was to walk downstream to Watersmeet where I could get a coffee and then fish back up. I would cross the river at the little ford and follow the footpath down the right hand bank.

The ford lies across the tail of a very tempting pool and I was unable to resist a quick cast there. A large rock offered helpful cover and standing behind it I fanned a series of casts across the pool but my mayfly imitation generated no response. Was it too early in the day for such a large fly, I wondered, or was the water too shallow and clear, the sun too bright? It really was a beautiful pool with bubbling water tumbling in at the head spreading to a wide apron studded with occasional grey rocks. Too lovely to leave too soon. So I crept out from my hiding place, surreptitiously edging forward to try a final cast to the very top of the pool.

As the fly landed at the side of the bubbles the water surface trembled, I flicked up the rod and felt a brief wiggle before the line went dead. It was fixed motionless. I had not seen a rise and should have been certain the hook was caught in a rock had I not definitely recognised that tiny moment of fishy wriggling. So I believed and held on and steadily exerted a gentle pressure. In the end he came out and my little rod bowed to him as he circled the pool, staying deep and serious. At last he came to the net and what a splendid trout he was – dark olive green mottled with bright chartreuse, generous black and red spots ringed with white. He might have been half a pound, perhaps, and he slid back into the water with a contemptuous wave of his tail.

The riverside path winds down the valley through ancient woodland dappled with flickering leaf-shadows and yellow flowers of cow-wheat twinkling under the trees. At Watersmeet House the lawns were busy with people having coffee and cake and my face lit with a smile for each of them, so everyone thought how nice and friendly I was, never suspecting the huge grins were not actually expressions of my delight in encountering such attractive interesting people but because I had just caught such a good fish.

Watersmeet House is a lovely place, situated opposite the confluence of the East Lyn with the Combe Park Water, hence its name. Built around 1832 for Walter Stevenson Halliday of the Glenthorne Estate as a romantic retreat and fishing lodge, it has been a tea room since 1901.

A man wearing a National Trust shirt kindly carried my tray of coffee and cake across the lawn while I took care of my rod and net.

"Have you had any luck?" he asked, putting my tray on a table near the river.

"Yes! I've had a lovely fish."

"Oh, well done. I used to go fishing on the Teme to catch those fish with bits dangling down here." He drew finger and thumb down over his mouth indicating a moustache. "Barbel?" I guessed.

"Yes, that's it, barbel. We used spinners. But most of the time we unintentionally caught eels."

I had to admit I knew little about spinning and had never caught a barbel nor an eel but Michael, as he introduced himself, was also interested in fly fishing and we fell into conversation. After a while he disappeared back into the house and reappeared with a fascinating haul – an armful of old fly rods!

"These were left here in the house," Michael said. "We don't know much about them."

They looked as if they had belonged to a party of Edwardian fishermen who had come in to this lodge tired and hungry after a day on the river and put down their rods at the sight of a pot of tea with scones, cream and whortleberry jam. Possibly there were also eggs and toast. It would have been a companionable meal with boasts of fish taken and commiserations for fish lost; memories cemented or embellished in the telling. And then perhaps some news arrived, maybe someone taken ill or died or a child born – a pressing need to leave in a hurry; or perhaps the certainty of an imminent return obviated the trouble of carrying extra luggage in the trap, the coach, the train. For whatever reason the rods were left behind with every intention of collecting them next time. But that never happened, maybe illness or war or some other trouble intervened, and here they waited still.

They were good quality rods and most were in sound condition. Some were of split cane with whipping every half an inch or so, one by Milward and another bearing the inscription 'The

De Luxe'. One rod of handful-thick whole cane with a green-heart tip section was over thirteen feet long and another, of solid red greenheart by Farlow in three pieces, fitted together with obliquely cut splices to reach an enormous nineteen foot six – salmon rods I supposed.

Claude Wade wrote of having two or three rods whose sections were joined with splices and said they were excellent rods and very light, but the long slanting splice sections must be bound together which he found rather a trouble, and they were inconvenient to carry the long distances he often walked to his fishing; so in 1875 he replaced them with a nine and a half foot three-jointed greenheart of Farlow's, which he used on small streams ever after. He also used a stiff twelve foot bamboo rod with upright rings, a fifteen foot rod by Forrest of Kelso and an eleven foot rod of Farlow's for peal, or sea trout. He disliked split cane which he found too whippy, preferring a rod with some stiffness halfway up from the butt. All the rods he describes sound much bigger and heavier than I would use and carrying them must have added considerably to the exertion of long days walking in this valley or over the moor. He wrote:

In a heavy flood you have to fish with tackle that could almost hold a whale in still water, because you can't run up and down the rocky and overgrown banks of the Lyn as you can on a garden lawn or the banks of the Wandle, and it's as well to have a 'stick' tough and stiff enough in your hands to back this tackle up, and to put a real strain on your fish upon necessary occasions.

Who were those long-gone fishermen who wielded these 'sticks', I wondered, and what fish did they catch? The dark patina of the sweat of their palms, slime of their fish, disasters and success of their days on the river, coated the rods in a deep chord of mystery.

Wade would surely have recognised the sort of rods we found here, would have been familiar with their heft and action and could have told us about the shortcomings and advantages of each. What he might have thought of my diminutive seven footer I cannot imagine.

Not far from the tea garden, a little below the meeting of the two waters, I found a wide saucer-shaped pool between open rocks. I crept towards it slowly, but the shallow skirt above the lip of a fall held several small fish and in the clear sunlit water it was impossible to avoid them seeing me; darting away with tales of outrageous intrusion, they doubtless alerted every other inhabitant of the pool to my presence. So though I hid behind a boulder to cast into deeper water at the middle and head of the pool, I was not really surprised when my Water Cricket elected no response. It was difficult to see this small dark fly amid the chiaroscuro of sunlight and shadow on the water's surface, so I changed to a Red Ant before slithering over rocks like a lizard to reach the next pool.

Small pockets of deep water nestled between a rubble of rocks and I cast into a few of these, keeping below the profile of the bank, half sitting on and half leaning behind a large boulder. On my third cast the water erupted, I lifted the rod and a bright bullet shape went into orbit on the end of my line.

'Bow to the fish', I remembered, was the proper thing to do when a fish jumps clear of the water – but it was hard. The trout was leaping and spinning in an energetic aerial display, only briefly touching the water as a springboard to gain more height for his next ascent. How could I maintain an even tension on the line when he was whipping it about so wildly? There was a heart-stopping moment of flash and splash and shattered silver when my little rod bent double over the foaming current and I felt sure he must come off. But he didn't; and after his spectacular air-borne flight above the pool he returned to his natural element and dived deep. By that time I had somehow fumbled the slack line onto the reel and could exert a little more control.

But the fish was only executing the second phase of his strategy with a new tactic more alarming than the first. Through the clear water I saw him take refuge under a rock and worried about him winding around its jagged edges, maybe breaking the line. So I applied some side strain, gently, persistently, and eventually managed to persuade him to leave by the route he went in, hoping to avoid tangles, only to see him turn and dart away in the direction of my pull to the next rock where he tried again. He circled the pool systematically diving under every rock he could reach.

Eventually he began to tire. The final two rocks he visited more slowly, more briefly, and at last came to my net. What a fish! Buttercup yellow belly, bronze-green back, heavy chocolate spots over his flank and a few scarlet ones towards his waist, each one haloed in light like the rings of a rise. He was stunning, and he slid from my hand back into the pool with a flick of his majestic tail and a spurt of undiminished energy.

On my way back upstream I fished a few likely looking spots, catching a trout here and there, and I wondered how much of this river would be recognisable to Claude Wade today. The 1952 flood must have shifted even massive boulders but the pools Wade loved to fish seem little changed from his description. Of course, the major pools dignified with names are really salmon pools and it was for salmon, and indeed salmon poaching, this river was most famous.

Salmon had their problems even in the nineteenth century. Wade describes how salmon in the River Lyn became sadly depleted as they were taken by 'snatching' or deliberate foul hooking and almost raked out of the river, this crime being at its height in the 1870s and early 1880s. On one occasion after a big flood he witnessed more than forty salmon caught within an hour by a dozen or so rods at Vellacott's Pool. Eventually, the good men of Lynton and Lynmouth resolved to take a severe line with poachers and snatchers, successfully allowing stocks some breathing space to recover.

Wade would certainly not have recognised the scarcity of salmon in the River Lyn today. Catch returns for this river in

2019, 2020 and 2021 were forty six, forty five and forty four respectively and in 2018 it was just eight. All but one of these fish were released unharmed. It is hard now to imagine the excitement of fishermen and vitality of the river as Wade knew it when he wrote, 'after a heavy flood in September or October, the salmon rush in more or less large numbers up the stream from the sea.'

Wade would have walked (and occasionally waded) this way often. A distinguished figure in tweed breeches, nailed boots and a bowler hat with two or three gut collars wound around it; those early leaders that had to be soaked before use and were best kept in loose coils around a hat band where, on a damp day, Exmoor mizzle kept them moist and soft. His determination to avoid everything new and bright such as a new well-polished rod, a new basket, and above all new shining brass fittings on either, would have ensured he remained inconspicuous to fish as well as refining his understated, if eccentric, dignity.

CHAPTER 15

Badgworthy Water

———

Badgworthy Water has its beginning in the wet lands of Lark-barrow and Tom's Hill where those ruined farmhouses, reclaimed by the moor, sit on the narrow watershed between Badgworthy and Chalk in the heart of Exmoor Forest. Here, numerous little trickles drain from the bog and, combining their forces, become runnels, rivulets, and eventually an infant streamlet running almost due north. I don't know which of its tiny tributaries carries the name of Badgworthy Water or where it could be said to truly begin. I wonder whether anyone does. It is joined by little streams draining from Pinford Bog and Buscombe, on either side of the delightfully and encouragingly named Trout Hill. Then Hoccombe Water comes in and the streams from Clanna Combe, Hoccombe Combe, Lankcombe and Land Combe, to run through Brendon Common and on into the little pastures at Malmsmead where Badgworthy Water joins Oare Water, and the combined streams become the East Lyn.

Badgworthy Water was made famous by Victorian writer R. D. Blackmore whose novel, *Lorna Doone*, was set partly in this valley which has been referred to as the Doone Valley and visited by legions of tourists ever since. Partly because of its associations with the book (and several films, of course) and partly, no doubt, because it has the easiest and prettiest moorland footpath it is a popular spot.

In that romantic tale, John Ridd met Lorna Doone as a result of fishing Badgworthy Water which was described as being 'as full of fish as of pebbles'. John set out to catch some loaches, as he had learned to do in the River Lowman when at school in Tiverton, and explains how it was done using a three-pronged fork firmly bound to a rod with cord. The well camouflaged loach tries to escape by hiding and must be speared by holding the fork lightly and 'allowing for the bent of it, which comes to pass, I know not how, at the tickle of air and water.' He describes how to steal up behind a loach to spear him as he lies facing upstream, 'in spite of the wry of the water, and the sun making elbows to every thing, and the trembling of your fingers.' But it doesn't always work and sometimes, just as you think you have him, 'lo! in the go-by of the river he is gone as a shadow goes, and only a little cloud of mud curls away from the prong he should have been on.'

I love Blackmore's description of fish-hunting, both for the language and because it reminds me of how, as a child, I used to catch mollyheads, or bullheads, by hand. John Ridd caught trout, minnows and very fine loaches in Badgworthy Water, though not as large as those in the Lowman, he said, where they reached a quarter of a pound. Of course, *Lorna Doone* is fiction but Blackmore knew intimately what he described so evocatively. When his father was curate at Culmstock, Blackmore fished the River Culm enthusiastically and was educated at Blundell's School so his descriptions of the school and the River Lowman which flows beside it are drawn from personal experience.

Claude Wade wrote his book of *Exmoor Streams* some thirty years after Blackmore's romance was published, his memories reaching back to the days before the novel's popularity brought tourists seeking the land so attractively described, and whilst he found the increasing numbers of tourists irritating I wonder whether he ever considered that his own descriptions of the moor and its waters are also very attractive indeed, perhaps bringing further tourists thronging to the still unspoilt land. And, I suppose, every book generating enthusiasm for remote places poses a degree of threat to their wildness and to the very qualities it celebrates but, at the same time, a greater understanding and appreciation of such places encourages their protection.

Upstream from Malmsmead I walked through small, sheltered fields just as Wade described, to the small farmhouse he remembered had once been called Cloud but, to his exasperation, was then known as Lorna's Bower. I feel sure he would be relieved to find that it is now Cloud once again. He explains that although there is some nice water in the meadows, most of it is heavily overgrown with bushes and so rather difficult and hardly worthwhile tiring yourself over with the whole of the Badgworthy Valley before you. I peered down into a few of these deep, shady pools between bushes but took his advice and walked up the meadows without trying to fish, anticipating the valley ahead.

The stream just above Cloud has some very attractive looking pools that must surely hold fish, but was rather busy with people paddling and picnicking. Wade complained of that stretch being not so easy to fish as it used to be in the old days before tourists came to look for John Ridd's water-slide. The water-slide is still there of course, though, in a perfect example of life imitating art, it seems a pale imitation of the one described so dramatically in the novel.

I walked up the footpath past the memorial to R. D. Blackmore, past the campsite on the far bank and past the floodgate before beginning to fish. Although the footpath was fairly busy all the way along, numbers thinned the further I went. I don't have sufficient confidence in my fishing to enjoy an audience but everyone I met greeted me pleasantly and made interested enquiries about my success.

Under the oaks in Badgworthy Wood I sat on a rock to chew some chocolate and watch the river. Several small, pale coloured flies fluttered above the stream so I tried a Deer Hair Sedge fly which sat up well on the water and just might look a bit like one of them. Under the left bank, where roots hung over the water, I rose a fish and missed it. I changed the fly and tried the spot again but he wouldn't give me a second chance. A wren skipped about the mossy bank watching me and doubtless found it amusing. I tried a few more shady pools where dark water bubbled between rock but had no further interest there.

Across the river I walked up a path following a seam between the moorlandy smell of sun-warmed bracken along the riverbank and the resinous scent of conifers in Deer Park Plantation. At the top end of the plantation I emerged onto moorland and sat on the riverbank to eat some lunch. A grey wagtail hopped from stone to stone, humming a cheerful tune in his head and tapping the time with his tail.

Back from the riverside were untidily shaggy clumps of rushes and unmade beds of bracken but the sheep-nibbled bank was like a lawn spangled in yellow tormentil. Eating my cheese, fruit and oatcakes I watched the water but could see no fish rising. Nevertheless, several pools looked tempting and I tried a few casts there but with no response. Perhaps I should have tried a nymph but in the shallow water it wouldn't actually have been a great deal lower. If the fish aren't rising I must make them rise, I thought. Is that possible to do? Perhaps sometimes it is.

Under Badgworthy Lees water hissed over stone, answered by the whisper of oak and birch while wind sighed through the grasses. A series of little pools looked very trouty so I crept through tangled bracken and slid into the edge of the stream to sit on its bank at the foot of the nearest one and, from there, cast towards the head of the pool where bubbling water tumbled in between stones. At last a nice little trout fell to my Deer Hair Sedge, small, but as bright and lively as the sparkling stream.

In the next pool I repeated the exercise with what I first thought was the same result. But when I drew the fish in it was not a trout but a salmon smolt of brightly polished silver freckled with pewter. Its face, even at that young age, was more finely featured, more aristocratic, than a trout's; and this creature I held in my hand, barely seven inches long, was something of a miracle.

From a redd of 2,000 to 2,500 eggs, only around thirty fry survive to become smolts and less than four will grow into adult salmon. Born in this Exmoor stream, this little fish spent its youth (is parrhood a word?) darkly dappled to hide from otter and heron amongst tawny pebbles or to lie unnoticed in the shade of overhanging oak and fern. Now its body had undergone profound transformation – in the process of smoltification it had readied itself to leave its moorland home beginning an adaptation from life in freshwater to one of salt, its colours changing to those of sunlight glinting on rolling wave, in preparation for a life at sea.

From our land-walking, air-breathing world, an underwater life feels alien and whether the water is fresh or salt seems of little significance. Yet, for a fish, the difference between life in fresh water and sea water is extreme. Osmosis is the tendency for water to pass through a semi-permeable membrane from a weak solution to a strong one, until the two are equalised. Cells submerged in a solution of higher concentration than their own will lose water and shrivel; cells in clean water will absorb water, swell tight and potentially burst. Imagine what this means for a fish.

In a river, the fish's body is saltier than the water around it so water is absorbed through its skin. It compensates for this by producing very dilute urine and absorbing salts through its gills. When it goes to sea, the fish will swim in seawater which is saltier than its body and it will lose water through its skin. To avoid a dangerous build up of salts in its body, the fish must excrete a strongly salty urine and expel salts through its gills.

Adjusting from one environment to the other requires profound physiological change and this does not happen simply as a response to the conditions a fish finds itself in, but begins whilst still in the river of its birth, its body actually becoming less suited to its home water in preparation for a journey not yet begun. A transformation I find truly miraculous.

I released the smolt to continue on his way to the ocean, wished him luck in his travels and walked back from the water to sit on the grass at the foot of the cleave. A couple of ravens flew over, croaking conversationally, and circled the breeze. Above them, higher and even higher, swallows gathered in preparation for a journey of their own, catching slanting sunlight on the points of their rapidly flickering wings.

CHAPTER 16

Badgworthy Crossing

A harsh kraark echoed around the valley as a grey heron lumbered away on broad wind-scooping wings. The steep sided hills were clothed in a tweedy mix of green bracken, yellow gorse and purple heather, with grasses turning a creamy gold, some of the bracken fronds burnished to copper and here and there the land was spotted with scarlet berries of hawthorn and rowan.

The lower reaches of Badgworthy Water around Malmsmead and Cloud are frequently busy but crowds seldom venture far from a road and I saw no more than a couple of walkers in the headwaters of this remote moorland valley. Wade wrote of how it was easier to catch fish in the old days, before tourists came to look for the land of Lorna Doone meaning, presumably, before 1869 when Blackmore's novel was published. However, the pilgrims of popular literature seem not to have caused him nearly so much trouble as he suffered from other fishermen.

Wade was concerned that in the open below Badgworthy Wood he was too visible to any other fisherman following him up the water and that, if the other was shrewd, he would slip past and begin fishing in front of him. Then, recently disturbed trout would be hiding instead of feeding and would not rise readily to his flies. So he liked to get away around the corner, out of sight above the wood, before he started fishing.

Today, larger rivers such as the Exe, Barle and East Lyn are fished at a reasonable level but are seldom as crowded as that and on small moorland waters such as Badgworthy I have never encountered another fisherman nor even heard anyone talk of fishing there. I am quite certain these waters are fished far less than they were in those hungry Victorian days when every trout was a much needed meal and monstrous catches were celebrated.

It was here, on Badgworthy Water, that Robert Freke Gould, Rector of Stoke Pero, once caught so many trout he had to hire a boy with a horse to carry them away. He had been born in the rectory at Luccombe and followed his father into the church, acting for a time as his curate. A keen and obviously skilled fisherman who made his own flies, he was a strong man of considerable stature and must have had the physical endurance to fish for a grindingly long day to achieve that famous catch of over 300.

Wade goes on to report how all the little streams flowing into Badgworthy Water had been full of trout, but frequent worming and 'groping', or tickling, by the locals had very considerably depleted them. Constant overfishing would certainly have a detrimental impact on populations but a half pound spawning trout is capable of producing 375 to 500 eggs so when pressure eases, all else being equal, numbers should quickly recover. Nowadays there must be far less fishing on Exmoor waters and catch and release has become a usual practice so few, if any, trout are taken by fishermen. However, numbers never seem to reach the levels of abundance Gould must have encountered and Wade and Blackmore describe.

Badgworthy Crossing is a ford for hoofed travellers with a footbridge alongside it for booted ones. A stone under the bridge, pale and peaked like an alp, always holds spraint from a passing otter; it has done so for years, layer upon layer of smeared records of all the otters who have passed this way. The name 'Badgworthy Crossing' is spoken by travellers over land who refer to crossing the river, but is just as relevant for otters travelling waterways who cross the track at this place.

The water was the colour of ale but tasted as fresh and clean as the wind blowing over the moorland. Bright sun glinted metallically off broken water. I cast a small olive with two long tails into the pool under the bridge and there was a rise and I missed it because I could not see the fly in the shimmering reflections of light. It didn't matter; there was so much more water to fish. I changed the fly for a similar pattern with a sharp green post, hoping it may be more visible, and moved on upstream, exploring the water, listening to the merrily chattering current and searching for likely spots where trout may lie in small dark pools between waterworn rocks.

Just above the junction with Hoccombe Water a rocky outcrop stands sentinel between the two streams and a fallen rowan tree, leafless but rich with berries, lay across a deep pool. That would be a good place for a fish, I thought, and sat for a while on its prone trunk. A dipper came bobbing along and laughed at my vain ideas; the rowan protected the pool effectively – I should never get a fly under there.

I slipped quietly down the bank to sit on a grassy ledge and cast towards the little pool above. The first cast caught seed-heads of tall, tussocky grasses overhanging from the far bank. I tidied the fly and raised myself up a little until I was half standing, half leaning against the bank, anxious not to raise my profile but needing a little more height to reach over the grasses fringing the water. Twice I cast towards the white bubbling head of the pool and twice watched the fly bobbing back towards me. On the third cast there was a bubbly 'splip', I raised the rod with no more than a gentle flick of my wrist and the tiniest trout flew out into the grass and bracken beside me. He was hardly heavier than the fly, no longer than my fingers but perfectly formed and richly coloured as an adult trout. I scooped him out of the grass, he had already lost the hook, and dropped him quickly into the foamy pool at my feet. It was not his temporary loss of dignity that made me laugh, it was the furious, wriggling indignance in such a diminutive body.

The stream babbles merrily along beside the remains of a dry stone wall, the old Forest wall, marking the boundary of the Saxon hunting Forest of Exmoor; the flattish grey stones set horizontally where they had been laid, uncemented yet closely fitting, by some Victorian craftsman. Now no longer maintained, the wall is sinking into redundancy amid the bracken and, a few yards behind, its duty is assumed by a wire fence.

A couple of pools further along another trout, only a little larger than the first and just as richly coloured, fell to my small olive pattern fly. And as I fished my way along the stream more dark bronze-green trout, brilliantly spotted with vermillion and black were drawn from the peaty water. The stream is tiny here, no wider than the length of my seven foot rod, and tumbles along in a series of pools divided by rocks in green velvet moss. On either side of the deep valley, hills swell skywards and on Tom's Hill Barrows, to my left, a few sheep watched me in curious astonishment whilst on the flank of Badgworthy Hill the round rumps of Exmoor ponies glowed like conkers among the gorse.

I reached a place where the fence made a dog leg up over the opposite cleave, where remains of a bank held a few tall beeches and beyond them a little combe came down steeply from the west. There seemed to be a co-ordinated hatch of many species of fly rising out of the wet ground at the foot of Trout Hill. Some, I think, were stone flies with double pairs of wings, there were tiny ones that might be small olives, large ones with long, long tails and dense swarms of midges lifting out of the mire like spiralling smoke.

Amongst the contents of my fly tin I found a fly with a green metallic twist over the body, a red hackle and tiny knotted feather-fibre legs. It was about a size fourteen. Beside the tail of the next pool I knelt in dense bracken and cast the fly towards the pool head, watched it land just below the bubbles close to the opposite bank, and the instant it touched the water it was eaten ravenously by the biggest trout I had found that day. He seemed enormous in that small stream and must have been close to six inches.

The late afternoon sun slanting down the combe lit up clouds of flies of every size, glinting off chitinous shell, shining through diaphanous wing, highlighting each insect like a spark of fire against the darkly shaded hillside beyond. All of them rose and fell, spinning and dancing, in a dizzying multitude that filled the valley from the celebrating stream to the top of the soaring hill, flickering and twinkling like a galaxy of stars.

Tributaries of the Taw

CHAPTER 17

The River Mole

At the tail of a big bend there was a shilletty beach shaded by ash, alder and oak where the pool riffled out to swing the other way into a right hand bend below. I cast a Red Ant onto the top of the riffle and let it wobble down on the broken water, arcing around me into a bubbly shallow at its foot. Next, I repeated the cast a little further across, and then further again. On the fourth cast the fly was taken by a pretty little trout who came splashing to meet me and wriggled hastily back from my hand; a small but joyful beginning to a day of puffy white cumulous sailing on the breeze across a cornflower blue sky.

The River Mole begins life in the moorland combe between North Molton Hill and Darlick. From this Exmoor birth it runs through woodland and farmland, strengthened by the River Bray and the Crooked Oak where fertile soils and lush grasses bring dairy cows to sink drooling muzzles into its waters until, at last, it joins the Dartmoor bred River Taw on its dignified procession to sea in Barnstaple Bay.

The Mole ran just three small fields away from my childhood home. For me it was a place of escape and retreat, excitement and intrigue, of solace and inspiration; comfortingly familiar yet always fresh, constantly new. Long summer evenings, weekends and school holidays were mostly idled away in its company while cuckoo and curlew song bubbled through the valley. From the high branches of trees on its banks I could watch fish, kingfishers, wagtails and sometimes a group of red hinds who came through the woods on the far side to drink. Herons often stood in the current; gaunt grey sentinels watching for fish. I saw my first mink there; trickling along the bank, pouring himself over stones and under roots, finally looking up and fixing me with a piercing jet stare from eyes like needles. I did not know, then, of their destructive tendencies but could see at once that, though sleekly beautiful, this was a creature not to be trusted.

A slow pool in a shady bend was a perfect place to learn to swim; it didn't offer much length but, otter-like, I enjoyed rolling, twisting, floating, feeling the way the river carried me and swimming down to explore its depths. Afterwards I would roll in the grass to get half dry. For years my feet were unhappy in anything but flat leather sandals, worn mainly so that I could walk straight into the river, spend the afternoon wading about and drain sufficiently to be admitted to the house by the time I got home.

My earliest fishing was done on the Mole, but it wasn't fly fishing. My grandfather taught me the subtle art of quiet wading in the shallows, slowly slowly lifting stones, holding them still while the little puff of mud swirled away and visibility cleared. Often a bullhead, or mollyhead as we called them, would be lying in the hollow beneath a stone, to be snatched with a cat-like pounce and scooped up in my hands. It was instilled in me that the riverbed should never be disturbed and the lifted stone must be replaced exactly in its original position. I was always careful to do so.

Bullheads are bottom dwellers, mottled and banded in the colours of the riverbed, and feed at dusk, usually spending the day under a stone. Perhaps because of this habit I have never caught one with rod and line but they can be caught by hand if you're quick. I wish now that I had counted how many stones had to be lifted to find one – it wasn't many. Such a figure might have been an interesting measure of abundance directly comparable with the river today. These dumpy little fish named for their broad, flat heads are familiar characters always greeted with great affection but, today, trout were my quarry and mollyheads left behind with other childish things.

Water slid low and faintly murky over brown pebbles as I moved along the side of the slow pool where a few tails of weed hung lankly in the sluggish current collecting clusters of leaves and twigs. I fished up through the pool, casting into the bubble line and under the bank but nothing else responded so I climbed out of the river and sat within the embracing limbs of an alder to eat some chocolate and change my fly while a small bird tapped a measure in the branches overhead.

After a short break while a wagtail wagged his grey tail on a mid-stream rock and somewhere a thrush smashed a snail, I scrambled out of the alder and fished on up the river, casting into the bubble line, the creases and pockets of the convoluted current, searching for fish. I tried a Deer Hair Sedge, a Black Gnat, a Dulverton Destroyer, which is an emerger pattern designed to hang in the surface with a little sparkle on the hook and invented by Chris – but all the usually reliable flies got no response. In a little way I reached a run where a rocky eminence offered a shallow shelf to stand on and a deep chasm, water-cut around it, might have held fish of any wildly imagined size. Though narrow, it seemed bottomless.

So I tried trailing a nymph through the dark passageway, feeling certain there must be fish lying in there, and repeated this a few times. Eventually, as the nymph swung out from the deep channel it was followed by a curious trout who watched with apparent interest but declined to take it.

While the nymph was still attached to my line I moved downstream, casting across and letting the current carry it down, swing it around and pull it along briskly. One tentative tug was felt but nothing was hooked and then, on a small riffle, I caught another little brownie; not large but pretty and a fish is a fish, and any fish is always welcome.

My memories of growing up on the Mole are not all idyllic. One Saturday morning, having missed visiting for several days, perhaps hampered by homework or bad weather, I set off for the river looking forward to spending another day happily spuddling about in its waters. No limits of time or distance were ever imposed on my roaming and it's sad to see how few children enjoy such freedom today. But all was not well in the river-run valley and I have never forgotten the shock of what I found.

Some vandal, some mindless, heartless thug with a bulldozer had obliterated the river. I could not believe what I was seeing, could not understand how anyone could . . . why anyone would. The devastation was horrifying.

The course of the river had been straightened, the bed raked level, banks regulated, every stickle, shallow, pool and bend obliterated in a mechanical sweep of destruction. In this magical place where I would not have presumed to displace one pebble, every feature of interest had been removed; small islands, sheltering rocks, stony beaches, holes in the banks and stands of waterside plants – gone. What remained was not a river but a lifeless canalised water conduit. A drain.

Routine dredging used to be considered good river management. Straight rivers occupy less space than wandering ones and it was thought that straightening and deepening a channel to carry water off the land and away to sea faster would reduce flooding. Between the Second World War and the late 1980s water authorities dredged rivers regularly.

Thankfully, this systematic practice has largely become a thing of the past. It is now understood that dredging rivers can destabilise their banks, causing erosion and siltation for some distance above and below the dredged section, and can actually make downstream flooding worse. Flood management today generally only uses dredging as a limited and targeted measure, preferring to find ways to slow the flow of water, rather than speeding it up allowing an uncontrolled rush into catastrophe. Much has been learned about fluvial processes and unintended consequences of interference. Perhaps we have also learned some respect for the communities of small, wild lives occupying rivers. I hope so.

The River Mole has suffered more than its share of injury and disaster, and has not escaped agricultural pollution. There have been times when its stones were furred in algae and pale-bellied dead fish washed up along miles of its banks. In one incident caused by mismanagement of anaerobic digestate, some 15,600 fish were killed including trout, salmon, bullheads, stone loach and minnows, with whole populations wiped out over three miles of river.

Much has changed in the valley of the Mole since the shorts-and-sandals summers of my youth. Curlew and cuckoos have long gone but the once rare otters have returned and previously absent roe deer are now common. The river has rebelled against its straightening, swaying in its chains, and begun to carve itself a newly sinuous course, to re-establish pools and riffles and islands, to wriggle free. Rivers are fluid in more than the obvious way, their waters constantly replenished, their courses constantly flexing; synonymous with change, their dynamic spirits are not easily restrained yet remain vulnerable to harm. In England today not one river is clean of chemical pollution. Not one.

Further along the river, far upstream, a pool lies under the left bank, not large but quite deep, where the river has curled itself into a hollow of the bank and hidden below a cluster of long hazel stems bowing overhead, some standing erect, some reaching more than halfway across its course and some almost skimming the water. From a fern fringed alcove enclosed within the arch of stems the rippling rings of a rise dilated across the pool.

On the opposite side the river had pared away the edge of the grass field to leave a vertical earth face just a few feet high; I bent almost double to keep my head below its horizon as I crept as close as I dared and crouched in its cover. For a few minutes I was still, hoping any perceived movement would be forgotten, letting my pulse steady, feeling the coolness of the water, listening to the chanting current, smelling the soft summer chord braided from green scents of herbs and grasses on the warm air. The fish rose again.

There was very little space between the surface of the water and the lowest hazel bough. My cast would have to be flat and accurate; if it splashed the water or caught in the bush all would be lost. I doubted I could do it.

What insects the fish was taking were too far away to be seen so I watched those around me, hoping to imitate what I was unable to name, and decided to use a very small, beige Deer Hair Sedge. After tying one on to a fine tippet I looked again at the narrow slot of space I must cast into and took a deep breath. It was tight.

I have no recollection of how I made that cast, having mentally closed my eyes to avoid seeing the inevitable disaster. But to my amazement it worked. My fly sailed under the low hazel bough to land softly in the middle of the pool, there was a quick splip of a rise and I flipped the rod tip sideways into firm contact with a solid and energetic fish. The trout swirled around the pool as swallows swirled looping and dipping over the meadow and when he came to my net he was as glorious and bright and vibrant as the cornflower-blue summer day.

CHAPTER 18

A Clear Water Stream

The opportunity to rent a cottage with two miles of trout fishing brought Henry Williamson to live at Shallowford in 1929. Williamson was a prolific writer but it was the success of his best known book, *Tarka the Otter*, that enabled him to move from the village of Georgeham to the four bedroomed thatched cottage on the Fortescue Estate. He already knew of the estate as one of the landowning family, Sir John Fortescue, whose *Story of a Red Deer* Williamson much admired, had written the introduction to *Tarka*. Leaving Georgeham was partly motivated by that village being 'written out', as Williamson put it, meaning either that he had exhausted the material he found amongst its inhabitants or that they were tired of being written about. But it seems the strongest draw was a dream of recreating his happy boyhood memories of coarse fishing, from the days before youthful innocence was shelled away in the trenches of the Somme.

On his arrival Williamson knew little about fly fishing for trout or salmon but by the time he left, eight years later, had learned much through reading, seeking advice and his own experience of fishing, managing and restocking a trout stream. He had also become a purist dry fly fisherman and my favourite picture of him, where he appears less writer than fisherman, is the portrait painted by Edward Seago in which we see a man of lean, weathered features with eyes deep and dark as a moorland pool; he is dressed in a comfortably worn-in tweed coat with a few flies in the lapel, a pipe in his mouth and a fly rod in his hand.

During his years at Shallowford, Williamson wrote another successful book, *Salar the Salmon* and later, from diaries kept at the time, a book about his family, *The Children of Shallowford*, and a delightfully engaging memoir of fishing and river management about those days spent on the River Bray called *A Clear Water Stream*, published in 1958.

This book begins on the summer day Henry Williamson and his wife, Loetitia, first visited the cottage that was to become their home and explored the valley around it. They wandered into the deer park, stood on the ornamental stone bridge they later named Humpy Bridge and gazed into the water below where trout lay idling in the stream. Williamson was instantly captivated by the place which rekindled memories of his past and held exciting promise for the future, and he wrote, 'Water, mysterious water, was speaking to me again.'

Fishing on this stretch of the River Bray is in private hands and not normally available to the public so I was enormously grateful for the privilege of being invited to fish here. I, too, arrived on a glorious summer day and it seemed fitting that, like Williamson, I should begin my explorations on Humpy Bridge from where I could see the cricket pitch on one side and the valley of the deer park on the other. I looked between jagged stones topping the parapet into the pool below. It was a substantial pool, out of all proportion to the size of the little stream, and in its green depths three or four dark shapes swayed in the current. As I watched they occasionally changed places, rotating in some mysterious aquatic dance choreographed by the river. I couldn't be sure of their size as in the dusky clear water it was difficult to judge their depth, but they looked big.

The enchantment Williamson felt for the place was at once infectious and my plans to fish upstream from the bridge were hastily revised in the face of such temptation. I slipped down the right bank to stand on a submerged section of collapsed walling and cast a peacock herl nymph into the pool a few times. This was duly ignored so, wondering whether it was getting far enough down, I tried a few casts with a hare's ear nymph with a heavy tungsten bead head. On one occasion the nymph was followed back towards me, but by only a little fish, and after a closer look was politely declined. Of the large fish there was no further sign. I scrambled out onto the grass feeling, if ever so gently, subject of the river's amusement.

Undismayed, and not really surprised, I walked on up the stream where shallow, shilletty beaches regularly exchanged sides with steep, alder and hazel clad banks, both graced with oak and ash trees of venerable age. I changed back to a dry fly, a green drake French partridge mayfly which had worked only the day before on the Batherm so perhaps might work here, I thought. A few mayfly were coming off the water, not many but they appeared large and the shucks drifting on the current confirmed it. One was carried by a wren, its wide pale wings protruding from the tiny beak as the bird flitted between prickly hawthorn branches making no attempt to eat it but probably planning to take the meal home to a nest of chicks as soon as I stopped watching.

The day was bright, the water of the stream as clear as Williamson's words immortalised it and, whatever the difficulties of fishing in such conditions, it was undeniably glorious. I flicked my fly into the dappled shade under an ash tree a few times and it was soon met by a small splip, a sparkling splash and a quick ash-leaf shaped shard of mirrored sunlight as I drew in a pretty little trout. He was light gold and silver, dotted with ink and vermillion, as clear and bright as the day.

When Williamson took over this water it had been heavily over fished and he restocked it from the fish farm at Exebridge with a mixture of native brown trout, a strain of trout from Loch Leven and salmon from the Tay. Under his care the fish apparently thrived and he regularly fed them with a proprietary fish food consisting of a mixture of broken dog biscuits and dried, shredded horse flesh, with wasp grubs when he destroyed a nest and, in a strange reversal of fates, even on herons, a couple of which he shot to protect his fish from their predations. Williamson was untroubled with concerns about maintaining the genetic integrity of his wild fish and I am unsure to what extent such matters were understood in those days. I wondered whether those stocked fish had left their mark on fish in the river today, and whether any distant ancestors of the little trout I caught had swum in the wide waters of Loch Leven.

The next section of river had been straightened at some time and fitted with a series of shallow weirs. As I reached the first of these I heard the motor of a mule buggy on the far bank so stood up and waved as Brian Mitchell, the head keeper, came trundling along with a wide grin.

"Wait there, I'll come round," he shouted across and drove down to Humpy Bridge and back up the right bank to meet me. Brian is cheery and pert eyed, always has a smile on his round face, always a joke on his lips.

"There's some fish about. Ed came down last week and caught four!" he told me. "I've never been into fishing but it looks very calm."

"It is not always calm," I said. "It can be really fun or it can be hugely frustrating. Usually frustrating."

I asked Brian about his pheasants and he told me how the first batch of poults had already gone to wood and more were arriving next week.

"They should be happy in this weather," I said, and we talked of the dry summer, game crops and the need for rain.

"Well you have a good day, I'm off to watch the rugby. And if you catch a salmon I shall give you a kiss!"

I assured Brian it would be worth risking a kiss to catch a salmon but I thought that unlikely and he revved up his buggy and roared away.

CHAPTER 19

Wheel Pool and Fireplay

———

Below the first weir, water under the far bank was deep and dark in a back eddy, slowly revolving and spotted with white bubbles spluttered out by the tumbling fall. It would be almost impossible to put a fly onto that glassy surface without the line dragging in fast water but I knew it would be an ideal place for a fish to lie, relaxing in slack water whilst watching for food being brought down on the current. When line falling across the middle of the stream was carried down in the strong water the fly would be dragged over the still pool creating a vee of ripples that no fish would ever mistake for an insect but these little trout were quick and perhaps if the fly was only there for a second it might be enough. I had to try.

So I cast across the stream and the fly landed in the slack water and by chance (I don't know how I did it) the line fell in a bit of a loop upstream and while the current gathered it together with every intention of snatching it away, the fly and the fine leader slowly twirled around with the bubbles. I watched the fluffy mayfly sitting up on the smooth water and just as the tautening line was about to drag it away the fly was sipped in, I lifted the rod and the current struck at the same moment and he was on! As I drew him across the river I felt the weight of a fairly solid fish and when he came to hand he was a beautiful plump trout of about eight inches. With a short chuckle a dipper whizzed down the stream.

Along both sides of the river, thick swags of water-crowfoot or ranunculus were flowering in the stream, as generous and lacy as the cow parsley along road verges. Williamson describes how, on the road between London and Devon, he stopped on a bridge over a chalk stream where the air was white with mayflies and, in the clear water, impressive trout of three or four pounds lay between bunches of white-flowered weed. Examining the plants, he found they held an abundance of invertebrates and decided they were just what he needed for the Bray. He bought two buckets from the nearest village shop and filled them with weed to take home. As soon as he got back he planted it in the river, anchoring roots with stones, spacing them in different runs and eddies.

Williamson realised that the nymphs and eggs of invertebrates transported in the weed from their chalk stream home were unlikely to survive in the acidic water of the River Bray but was confident the weed would offer holding for the local nymphs, and so provide more feed for trout. His efforts earned the scorn of taproom 'experts' who assured him the plants would be washed out in the first spate, but they were not. In fact, every spate spread the weed further by breaking off pieces and carrying them downstream to lodge against stones where they readily took root. He noticed how the stems trapped silt which built up around them, bringing security and nourishment to the roots. The growth became luxuriant.

Greenery covered half the area of the river before doubt was initiated by a visitor who said that *Ranunculus fluitans* was a weed of chalk streams where the flies were different to those of rapid moorland waters. Here, the local nymphs lived under stones and ate the algae which grew on them but now those stones were being shaded and smothered below rampant weed. It was pointed out that the cost of damage to the value of fishing rights, on that estate and downstream all the way to the sea, could be enormous.

Williamson became worried. He couldn't sleep. Panic set in. He got up at 3 o'clock in the morning and worked until midnight on the gargantuan task of digging out the weed but never succeeded in eradicating it. Despite carrying away armfuls of greenery, the roots had wormed their way deep into the substrate of the river and could never be entirely removed. We should never forget how easily a species can be introduced to a habitat and how difficult, often impossible, it may be to eliminate. The plants constantly grew back.

And here they grow still, their long tresses combed by the current, white and yellow floating flowers scattered with damselflies, bringing to the stream a pre-Raphaelite romance quite in keeping with its gracious parkland setting. They do not appear to have a detrimental impact on the river which holds plenty of fish. Insects are attracted to the flowers and aquatic invertebrates to the submerged greenery, so fish benefit from food and cover the plants provide. Yet perhaps of even greater value is their role in diversifying the flow of water and influencing the arrangement of the stream bed. As Williamson noted, the plants trap silt which builds up around them becoming little islets at times of low water and squeezing the flow into narrower, deeper runs between clumps where the speed of current keeps the gravel clean. Clean areas are needed by spawning fish, silty areas by invertebrates such as damselfly and mayfly nymphs. The health of a river habitat is optimised by a balance of both.

I sat on the bank to eat some chocolate. Jewel coloured damselflies fluttered between tall grasses and an elegant green-bodied spider (and for me to appreciate a spider it must really be very elegant indeed) with tan coloured legs, smooth and supple as a thoroughbred, lay languidly below a finely-spun trapeze web. Over the water a mayfly danced her courtship to the stream.

Above the straightened section the river wanders again at will and, in its freedom, describes an extravagant S bend forming two deep pools, the lower of which Williamson named Wheel Pool because a large part of it was in eddy, with water turning back under the far bank canopied by oaks in a dim green shade. In the low water conditions the eddy was partly dry and Williamson had noted gravel and sticks deposited there by floods, as they were that day, but with higher water levels the eddy could easily occupy a third of the pool, as he described.

Through the pool's centre the rock was split into deep fissures, falling away into shadow. There must be fish in there, I thought, but nothing moved except the swirling current. Nothing was induced to rise by my mayfly and I decided, if there were fish there they must all be too deep to react to a distant fly far above them on the surface. So I tried a nymph; a gold headed hare's ear, teased loose to give it a little leggy movement, with a fine gold rib and a scant pheasant tail wisp. I cast across the pool from the inside of the bend and let the nymph drift back through the first deep fissure. I caught a stick, dragging it out from the bottom, sodden and heavy. Trying the next deep channel, I saw a fish come to examine my nymph. He didn't take it and he wasn't very big but he was there and he was interested, which was encouraging. With the following cast I caught another stick. I tried again.

My nymph landed on the far side of the slow pool, glinting for a moment as it sank through a shaft of sunlight piercing the unfathomable darkness. Slowly, a huge torpedo-shaped leviathan of a fish rose from the shadowy depths of the fissure and my breathing stopped. The great fish followed the nymph, examined it and turned contemptuously away. If he had had a middle finger, he would have raised it. With familiarity of the dismal, my normal breathing resumed.

That pool held no further promise so I moved along the foot of the bank. A great mound of gravel had been scraped up by broad paws in the habit of otters known as 'castling' to create a pedestal upon which to display a spraint, elevating it to a prominent position from where its scent will be carried across the bend on the prevailing wind; a clear sign which no other otter could miss, announcing ownership of territory in otter language. The spraint it held was the largest I had ever seen – long, sixteen-bore diameter curls folded into the gravel. Tarka, I thought, was alive and well in the valley.

Williamson was told that every spring otters bred in a stick pile at the side of this pool and he removed the sticks to encourage them to breed elsewhere in an effort to protect his fish. However, they cannot have gone far as he also found gravel kicked up here, a discarded trout tail on a stone and the remains of an otter-predated salmon at the edge of the pool above. When he bought 250 young trout to rear on in a pond and all but three were taken by otter, Williamson philosophically set the loss against his royalties from *Tarka*.

The next pool was on the reverse bend so I dragged a stick from flood debris in the bank to help me across the river to the shallow side. Williamson called this Fireplay Pool because it was just below the viaduct on the Taunton to Barnstaple railway line and when a late steam train passed over in the evening, he watched the play of fire on steam reflected in the water. In those days, jackdaws roosted under the sleepers and bees nested among the ribs of the high steel and wooden structure, smudging the valley with the scent of honey as it dripped and drooled stickily to the ground. The railway is long gone but the viaduct remains and, in a triumph of Victorian engineering, the same towering stone pillars now support an angular concrete structure carrying the North Devon Link Road. Whilst passing trains must have been an occasional intrusion the drone of traffic today is unremittingly constant. I wondered, too, what impact those clouds of exhaust fumes might have on the insect life of the valley and stream.

In the clear sunlit water I could see fish holding station so, presumably, they could see me, but I lurked in the shade of an alder hoping I was not too obvious. I tried another French partridge mayfly pattern, of natural colour this time, and was sure it floated across the pool nicely, having landed softly and travelled at the same speed as the bubbles. It sat up on its hackles and looked perfect, but when it had passed over three fish, none of which were spooked but all of which ignored it, I knew it was time for a change.

Williamson used a Poacher, a fly described as a jolly little fellow of red game cock hackles tied with gilt wire and three whisks which was particularly recommended for low water. I found a small red fly roughly answering that description with fine gold rib giving it a subtle sparkle.

From the cover of shady branches which raked my hat and snaggled the net on my back, I cast the fly out towards the nearest fish first without result and then, extending line each time, reached progressively further across the bright, smooth pool. My third cast stretched close to the foot of the steep, earth bank near the top of the pool and as it landed it was snatched by a small trout who leaped into the air and sped around the pool, sparkling in the sunshine. So I drew him in, and as he shimmered from my fingers back to the welcoming stream I thanked him for restoring my confidence.

Reaching the cottage at the head of the valley I was pleased to find the river returned to a state of dignity; it is no longer used as the domestic rubbish dump it was when Williamson found discarded bottles, tins, egg shells, potato peelings and coal ashes. This is just one river but I believe the improvement in attitude is widespread. Dumping rubbish in rivers was once common practice given little thought but, whether through respect for rivers or for regulatory enforcement, most people (except water companies, of course) would not deliberately and systematically do that now, offenders becoming infuriating exceptions rather than the depressing rule.

As shadows lengthened I heard no evejars, no curlews and no cuckoos as Williamson did, and whose calls formed the background music to my own local childhood yet have all fallen silent here today. Still, other birdsong lit the valley as I plodded along the track back towards my vehicle and a waiting cup of tea. I was tired and thirsty but at peace with the summer day, and I remembered that Henry Williamson walked this same path home, rod in hand, pipe in the corner of his mouth, to a singing iron kettle and tea beside his beechwood fire.

Eastern Waters

CHAPTER 20

Horner Water

———

Horner Water truly begins near Alderman's Barrow, where numberless drainings from Hurdle Down gather together to form a stream, known here by its maiden name of Chetsford Water. Wending its way through honey-perfumed heather moorland, joined by other streams from every combe and goyle, it becomes Nutscale Water for a time and pauses to fill a small reservoir before eventually assuming the title of Horner Water and plunging into the deep woods of Horner Valley.

After a few miles of twisting through oak woodland the river emerges at Horner Green where cottages of rough stone walls and wavy roof-tiles are the same mulberry red as the soil. Tall bean sticks stand over neat rows of vegetables and marigolds with murmuring bees and a quiet conversation of hens. Low garden walls, unable to contain the abundance, spill over with roses and lavender. Here, cream teas are served on tidy lawns and a farm shop sells honey, eggs, ice cream, meat and other local produce.

At West Luccombe Farm, a broad grass verge below shady beeches and limes seemed a perfect place to park my battered four wheel drive, where he felt agriculturally comfortable between a hay tedder and a roller. A red-rutted lane, warm with the resinous scent of stacked timber, led to a field of mowing grass alongside the river and, seven foot rod in hand, I set off to explore.

The river snaked along the eastern boundary of the broad meadow. Along its banks I crept through nettles, brambles and hemlock water dropwort growing tall and rampant in the rich red soil, stooping under low boughs of alder and sycamore to peer into its secluded course. It was small. Even at this lower end of the beat, which was only around a mile and a half from the sea, the broadest parts were no wider than a farm track. A six foot rod might have suited better.

A motherly old ash tree minded a pool, its roots embracing a tangle of unwanted sticks and discarded twigs of flood debris. From the pebbly shallows, I cast a Red Ant towards the base of the tree and at my second cast a fish rose from the dark water. I missed it. A couple more casts and I rose another with no greater success. I moved on to look for another pool.

Between holly and sycamore bushes, I found one. My first cast was halfway up the pool towards water bubbling in at the head. The fly wobbled down the centre of the stream for a couple of feet and was engulfed in a splashy rise with a flash of silver as the fish turned away but a quick flick of my wrist halted his escape and my line drew him back, inexorably, back to me. Though not much longer than my hand, he was a bright and beautiful little trout with parr smudges just fading from his sides.

Horner Water and the tributary River Aller were among the favourite rivers of William Thornton who became curate at Lynton and then the first incumbent of the newly created parish of Exmoor at Simonsbath. He was a lifelong friend of the Reverend Walter Stevenson Halliday of Glenthorne, who built Watersmeet House, and he also knew and had fishing lessons from Reverend Robert Gould, the famous catcher of that record basket of trout. While living at Selworthy as a student, between 1847 and 1849, he fished frequently and enthusiastically on these waters. In his 1897 *Reminiscences and Reflections of an Old*

West-Country Clergyman, Thornton wrote, 'I always had a liking for small and crabbed waters, for no one fished them; in them the good fish live, and are unsophisticated withal.'

Thornton generally carried a basket which held fourteen pounds weight of trout and did not consider that he had fished well if he did not succeed in filling it. He tells us that his trout averaged about eight to the pound and that his best catch of nine weighed collectively three and a quarter pounds. Well, at eight to the pound his fourteen pound baskets would have contained around 112 fish, so a very similar number to Wade's daily averages.

Gradually I worked my way along the stream where clear, golden water gurgled over mulberry red pebbles, sometimes walking the banks, sometimes dropping in at a likely looking spot, until I found myself back at West Luccombe Farm. Sparrows squabbled, swifts squealed wheeling over the yard and swallows swooped around farm buildings of the same red stone as the riverbed.

Opposite the farmyard, a bridlepath ford offered an easy entrance to the river and, just above the crossing place, a rusty iron gate stuck in the bank leaned drunkenly over a small pool where the surface was massaged by the churning current below. On the left bank an elder bush dangled its twigs over the water which, whilst not wide, looked pretty deep. In the dark water under the elder a fish moved.

From a discreet distance downstream, I cast towards it but could not get the line around the elder twigs so, sitting on low rocks under alder bushes on the right bank, I shuffled closer. A couple with a Labrador walked into the ford and stopped to say hello.

"Hello!" I called out, smiling back at them and wondering how I must appear, sitting in the mud under a bush at the side of this tiny stream. Most people grow out of that sort of thing when they leave primary school. My attention diverted, I momentarily forgot the tip of my rod with its fine two pound leader which was grasped (deliberately, it seemed) by a cone on an alder twig. It was impossible to detach. I had no idea how tightly and securely alder cones could grip on to thin monofilament line; they would make excellent indicators for nymphing, I thought, and it took several minutes of strained patience to release. When I had finally disentangled the troublesome cone, I looked back at the pool where the fish moved again. Perhaps it was fortunate that a tiny thing like an alder cone should make me stop and be still for a while.

Cast into the middle of the pool, my fly fell into water swirling with light. I couldn't see it in the brightness for a moment but I did see the tighter swirl of a fish and snatched the line, lifting the fly off the water too fast. It didn't connect.

Taking a deep breath, I tried again. A flat cast sent the line out below the bushes and the fly turned over but landed a bit further to the left than intended, in shallower water at the pool edge. As I was about to lift it off it moved in the eddy so I let it go and it circled around clockwise to drift into the top of the pool, and just as it reached the deeper water, Sploop! I snapped up the rod and felt a decent weight on the line. This was a good fish, I felt, as he circled powerfully, bending my rod over the little pool. He was a splendid trout of about nine inches, solidly built, pale bellied and dark backed with brilliantly spotted flanks and as he slid from my fingers back to the stream, I was quite sure, that angry flick of his broad scraper-shaped tail was defiance.

Further downstream, where Horner Water meanders through Porlock Vale on its way towards Bossington Beach and the sea, it is joined by the River Aller. Thornton wrote of how dearly he loved that 'woody, tangled brook' where he often fished with worms or bluebottles or sometimes, with infinite pains, using artificial flies and noted that its trout, if not numerous, were large and fat.

Earlier, I had visited a project run by the National Trust on one of the River Aller tributary streams. Ditches had been filled in allowing water to wander through a plashy meadow on routes of its own choosing, creating a network of runnels where it filtered through the sward between patches of marshy growth. Slowing the flow in this way was designed to lessen effects of drought or flood and as water seeped through grasses and rushes and infiltrated the soil, sediment and impurities would be filtered out so the river downstream should be cleaner. It was early days yet, and the project was due to expand, but I looked forward to seeing the results in the longer term and what changes this management might bring to the little river and perhaps to the girth of its trout.

A little further along the Horner at Burrowhayes Farm there are two bridges, a narrow high-arched packhorse bridge a few paces above a wider road bridge with a low Tudor shaped arch inscribed 'builded 1854'. There's always a fish under a bridge so, a little way below, I crossed the river as quietly as I could to reach shallow water along the right bank. A duck dabbling about in the margin was disturbed but, I hoped, nothing else. Caddis cases splattering the red riverbed pebbles were all tightly clustered into the downstream sides of stones, sheltering from the current which must often be more violent than it was that day.

With elder and holly at my back I cast towards the elegant stone bridge, aiming for the line of bubbles close to the opposite bank where a crudely pollarded ash trunk supervised the pool. The fly landed in dark water below the stone arch and just as it slid from shade to sunlight it was sipped in by another fine fish of eight or nine inches.

There is a campsite at the farm but a thick hedge secluded the river from the busy camp field, then a wooded stretch where water tumbled between mossy rocks and the shaded pools held some small but sporting fish and I caught a few more, and then a field of goats between the river and the road. And then I came to Horner Green.

In a wide, saucer-shaped pool below the cottages the stones of the riverbed changed colour from dull red to lightest gold. I could see fish plainly in the clear, shallow water and they, I supposed, could see me. I tried one or two surreptitious casts but they were not interested and I moved on.

There was more heavily shaded water between mossy banks where the river was steeper, faster, with rock-troubled white water between small dark pools. It was tricky to keep the fly in the slow water of the pockets behind rocks when the line had to fall across fast water to reach it. Nevertheless, I caught a couple of fish; on one occasion, the snatch of the current on the line helpfully making the strike for me at just the right moment.

I crept along under the bank towards Horner Bridge, its red stone clothed in moss and ivy, and settled on a low rock to cast. The fly sailed forward, under the pointed arch, to fall softly into the bubble line just the way I intended it to and I enjoyed a moment's satisfaction. It was a brief moment. The instant it landed a fish rose to it and I lifted the rod and I missed.

It had been a good fish and perhaps he was still there. He wouldn't take this fly again but perhaps if I changed it he might be tempted by something that looked different, I hoped. If he had a few minute's rest, perhaps. If I didn't move.

So I put on the most different looking fly I could think of – a Dulverton Destroyer. There was no reaction. I tried again. Nothing. So I crept forward to the stonework of the bridge and cast further up the shady pool below the arch. I made a few casts, extending more line each time to reach the little pool emerging just above the bridge. I tried the centre of the pool first, then the far right, then the left. The fly drifted further left in an eddy and I craned my neck to keep it in view. As it kept travelling I leaned forwards, peering around the corner of the stone abutment to watch it.

Cautiously, I stepped towards the centre of the stream, bending nearly double, but the fly kept moving to the left and just as I thought I had lost sight of it for good I saw a friendly little splash and with a quick lift he was on. The fish came to my hand, not very big but, oh, so welcome and very lovely, a light soft gold, the colour of the riverbed and of gentle sunlight through pale amber water, like Horner honey. There's always a fish under a bridge.

CHAPTER 21

The River Avill

———

Dunster Castle stands over the town's High Street with an air of authority but its far side looks down on parkland, meadows, trees and the little river at its foot with a relaxed elegance. The River Avill ran briskly as I explored its pools and riffles, walking downstream through fields below the castle with the idea of fishing upstream on the way back. There must be fish in here, I thought, and a kingfisher, slipping from an alder to shoot downstream, assured me there were.

The first accessible place was a streamy run between two over-hanging ash trees; neither deep nor riffly, it wasn't ideal but offered the first opportunity of getting a fly onto the water. It was doubtless due to my lack of confidence in the spot that I was not expecting a fish and the rise came as a complete surprise and I missed the strike. Still – it was encouraging to see there were fish in even the least likely stretches of this river.

Just around the corner I came to a very promising looking pool with, not a riffle exactly, but slightly faster water coming in at its head bringing a few bubbles into the dark green water. Those bubbles marked the ideal spot to place a fly but my eye was drawn to a place near the tail of the little pool where the bubble line curved under the ivy-hung bank. There was a narrow gap between a bushy sycamore and a spray of alder spreading low over the water like a steadying hand.

Could I get a fly into that tight space between branches I wondered, as I lifted the back cast awkwardly high to avoid the bank behind me and aimed a Red Ant fly towards the spot. To my delight it went in but drifted down towards the sycamore unsaluted. I tried again. On the third attempt I saw the silvery dart of a fish follow the fly, examine it and turn away. Then, undecided between discretion and greed, he came back for another look before finally, emphatically declining. The peaks and dips of my heart rate would have made an interesting pattern on a monitor.

As I retrieved my fly and dried it off I saw a rise just ahead of the alder. Surely a different fish, I thought, but couldn't be sure. The fly landed gently just above the spot, floated towards the leafy twigs and was sipped; I snapped the rod up but there was no fish. I was uncertain whether I had snatched too fast or the fly had been rejected but, anyway, decided to try a different one so opened my tin, wondering what to try next.

A small, grey, unassuming F-fly made from a duck feather seemed to want a chance so I tied a size sixteen on a fine tippet and dropped it into the short space between the bushes. It was accepted at once, I lifted the rod and felt a hefty fish whizzing strongly around the pool, snapping tension into the drip-flicking line. That was more like it! And then he came off.

Having reeled in line and dried the fly, I prepared to move on upstream but hesitated. That fish wouldn't take again but there might be another – had there been two? I wasn't sure, but just in case I cast into the narrow opening between the bushes once more.

The F-fly was met with an enthusiastic sploop and a good fish circled the pool on the end of my line, leapt clear of the water and eventually allowed himself to be guided into my net. What a spectacular trout; glittering gold and pewter, speckled with jet, though with very few red spots and those hardly red at all but more a polished mahogany brown. He must have been about a foot long and, fairly fat, must have weighed around three quarters of a pound.

When the fish had slipped back into the stream I tried another cast, just above the alder spray, more for the joy of the green-lit pool than in any real expectation of another. But there was another, and he readily took the fly and soon came to hand. He was almost as large as the first, just as plump and of similar metallic colouring. As I supported him in the reviving current, I thought what excellent fish this little river held.

A fallen log near the bank offered a convenient place to sit for a moment, to have some chocolate and admire the elegant landscape around me while overhead two buzzards and a red kite waltzed together in the summer sky. On a wooded prominence lifting high above the meadows, red stone towers and turrets of Dunster Castle rose serenely out of the trees. This had been the Luttrell family seat since the fourteenth century and here Claude Luttrell spent his boyhood in what he described as a sporting paradise; hunting, shooting and catching 'unlimited' trout in this river which loops around the castle on its way to join the Bristol Channel.

Born a younger son to a titled landowning family, Luttrell grew up to have the tastes and inclinations of a country squire without the income to support them. He was originally destined for the Church but quickly realised that such a modest way of life would not suit him and turned to banking, eventually becoming a director of Stuckey's bank. According to memories recorded in his 1925, *Sporting Recollections of a Younger Son*, that seems to have been a satisfactory arrangement, financing an abundance of country sport.

Luttrell quotes a record from 1904 when one rod caught ninety three trout in a day on the River Avill, many up to three quarters of a pound and a few just touching the pound, stating that in those days it was also possible to catch a sea trout or two but that numbers had diminished due to drainage operations preventing their free run up from the sea.

Of his own memories, Luttrell writes about some wonderfully good days on this river where, he says, the fish are larger than those on Exmoor. On his best day he caught 101 fish, including a good proportion of between half a pound and a pound. 'The biggest fish I ever caught at Dunster weighed two and a half pounds,' he wrote. 'I was fishing with very light tackle as the water was very clear, and a small fish took my bob fly, when suddenly, the big fish came out from under the bank and took the tail fly. Luckily I had a good deep pool to play them in, and after a quarter of an hour's very exciting work, I landed them both.' What fun he must have had, and so was I having, on this lovely water in its gracious setting.

It is unsurprising that fish would grow larger here than on the moor, even in streams of a similar size. The acid peaty water, harsh climate and rapid flow of high moorland streams offers much less food for fish than they might find in this fertile, sheltered land. Animals such as freshwater shrimps and snails, for example, cannot live in water without good levels of calcium for their shells. On the other hand, the lower reaches of a river are likely to suffer far more from human activity through siltation, pollution and physical restructuring. I had taken around an hour to catch two fish and had no chance of reaching a hundred in a day, yet it seemed there were, by today's standards, an excellent number of fish of a quite impressive size in the sporty River Avill.

Above Gallox Bridge I wandered further upstream, past a quiet stretch where water slid below tall alders and a weeping willow, where the banks were contained behind stakes, and on to fields above. There, the river twisted between peaceful pastures grazed on one side by sheep and on the other by Hereford cattle who gazed at me in bemusement from broad white faces. The river there was too overgrown to cast far, the water too clear and shallow to get close, but these are poor excuses for not catching a fish, because fish were there in plenty. I saw them scattering in front of me as I alarmed them.

I explored as far as Frackford Bridge, which carries the Tim-
berscombe road over the river, presumably replacing the earlier
bridge beside it on which an inscription was illegible but for
the name 'George'. Was this a King George, a George Luttrell?
I didn't know. The only sadness in this delightful place was the
rubbish in the river below these bridges; there was discarded
garden machinery, chunks of tiled masonry and even a projec-
tor screen. I tried hard, but failed, to understand the
desperation or ignorance of whoever had done such a thing.
People's level of respect for rivers is so disappointing sometimes
and I wonder that they cannot see their beauty, their joy.

It was interesting, though, to see two shoals of fish in this
stretch, where the river was secluded between thick hedges of
elm, alder and buddleia all bound together with bramble and
bindweed. Here the current ran along evenly uninterrupted by
rock or bend, the riverbed was of finer gravel and sand and
even, in some places, mud. One shoal included over eighteen
fish in parallel formation, all perfectly aligned with the current,
those at one end of the group dropping off and circling around
to join the other end, as starlings do in a flock. Occasionally
one of the number darted forward and rose to a fly, then hurried back into position in the ranks.

In the afternoon, after pausing on the way for a cup of tea, I
returned downstream to try one or two of the pools I had
missed earlier. The low lying pasture below the castle is known
as Dunster Lawns; the site of shows, country fairs and polo
matches. Specimen trees of majestic proportions grace the landscape – holm oak, pines, planes and poplars with massive trunks
wrapped in deeply fissured bark. As I walked along the riverbanks the Lawns were blackened with rooks who congregated
on the grass searching for leatherjackets and I thought it very
likely they were descended from birds Luttrell described watching from windows of the castle drawing-room where he looked
down into rooks' nests built in the tops of trees on the slopes.
Below the browse line of parkland trees, cars were visible on the

main road and whenever I left the soothing voice of the river, the sound of traffic, though distant, was a constant reminder of our times. Claude Luttrell would not have heard much traffic but I doubt the sound of the river, the gentle landscape and the scent of its trees and grasses has changed very much.

A short way below the Palladian Bridge, in making a sharp right turn, the river had scooped a large round pool with steep grass-fringed banks on the outside and a pebbly beach on the inside of a tight bend. A few alders and a shamble-limbed willow stood over the pool with one alder bough reaching down to hang just above the surface of the water. I sat on the pebbles from where a hilltop folly, Coneygar Tower, dominated the skyline on the far side of the pool and the river described a not quite complete circle around me. I tied on a size sixteen hare's ear nymph. The ideal place to cast it would have been at the foot of the white water tumbling into the pool but the alder bough made that impossible. But what if I cast into the fast water just above and let the current bring the nymph down over the rapids; perhaps the line could rotate around me and pass below the branch.

So that is what I tried and it seemed to work. I sat at the centre of the circle holding the line as it swung in an arc around me like lunging a horse and, in this way, caught a couple of pretty little trout parr. Then, through the taut line, my fingers felt stronger life on the end. I lifted the rod and an athletic fish exploded into action, leaping a couple of feet out of the water, flashing silver as he spun in the air, splashing back in a flurry of spray and leaping again. On the fourth leap he cleared the low alder bough like a bounding deer but as he dropped over the far side the line caught in twigs leaving him dangling for a moment like a Christmas tree decoration before he dropped off the hook into the pool, his freedom well earned by the amusement he brought. Even the watching castle seemed to chuckle, perhaps remembering similar escapades and the long-ago laughter of a young boy who once fished here.

The River Haddeo

CHAPTER 22

A Stream for Spring

At the foot of Bracken Bank Pool I sat amongst sere stems of last year's dock and bracken on the first day of the season, watched the water and wondered whether it was still too early to expect a fish to rise to a fly while feeling how good it was to be back with a little trout rod in my hand. The River Haddeo glowed with golden brown pebbles and bright emerald weed in clear water. A tiny parr with dark fingerprints along its flank drifted backwards down the stream. It paused beside me momentarily with a flick or two of its tail to hold against the current, dropped another step, paused again, and at last sank back to disappear tail first into waving tresses of weed. After a few minutes another one came down in a similar way, and then another.

The River Haddeo is a good stream for springtime. It rises close to the top of a field in the Brendon Hills, a spring welling up from yellow clay below a rough-barked elder, lifted by the vigour of its birth to swell proud of the earth. Where has it come from, this water that emerges so eagerly; how long has it been imprisoned in underground darkness before reaching this place to rise, clear and hopeful, wide-eyed into the daylight?

Whatever its early aspirations, in mid-life this river is amputated by the artificial impoundment of Wimbleball reservoir.

The lower river below the reservoir is therefore less subject to the natural spates and droughts of other streams and, possibly, as it is fed from deep water behind the dam, is also buffered from extremes of temperature. Anyway, the life of the Haddeo seems to awaken earlier in spring than life on other nearby rivers.

Although I watched the water for some time I could see no fish rising but nevertheless tried an experimental cast up the pool with a darkish Deer Hair Sedge that might look a little like a march brown fly, with a tiny gold headed hare's ear nymph hanging below it from the bend of the hook. On the third cast a fish rose to the dry fly with a small but enthusiastic splash. I struck too late, missed the fish and caught a tangle of dry stems on the bank instead. Even as I lamented my ineptitude I delighted in the knowledge that fish were awake and, if offered sufficient enticement, would rise. After retrieving and untangling my leader I tried again, fanning a series of casts across the pool but there was no further response.

A green eel came contorting across the river, moving in a series of bends, folding and refolding himself through the current. It was extraordinary to think he had travelled all the way from the Sargasso Sea to live here in the Haddeo. That weed-rich area of the northwest Atlantic Ocean, with no land borders, is held like a massive eddy within a swirling meeting of currents, and there all eels are born. We think. No one has actually seen a mature eel in the Sargasso Sea, or witnessed eels spawning, but it is from there that their larvae originate. In tiny transparent and barely visible forms, infant eels drift thousands of miles on the Gulf Stream to reach Europe where they become glass eels; clear slender creatures half the size of a pencil which swim up rivers to make their homes in freshwater. This one had come up the River Exe against battering currents and, unable to leap like a salmon, yet had somehow wriggled over or past impossible weirs to reach this stream where he developed size, colour and substance.

Wade writes that 'eels are terrible brutes to bother you and tangle up your line.' When fishing with a worm for salmon, he was always fancying he had bites, which came 'chiefly from the undercurrents, but often from trout, and more often still from eels.' So perhaps, in those days, eels were more common than trout. He considered the bites of salmon and eels to be easily confused; several times finding he had a salmon when he thought he was being bothered once more by eels, and tells of a fishing companion who was certain he had a good bite from a salmon and had hooked it until, to their disappointment, they saw a three pound eel come to the surface.

Today, I seldom encounter eels and not simply because I don't fish with worms nor because of their obscure nocturnal lives. It is estimated that numbers of glass eels reaching European coasts have fallen by ninety five percent over the last forty years and they are classed as Critically Endangered. Reasons are thought to be various including overfishing (smuggling glass eels is said to be more lucrative than smuggling cocaine), weirs, dams and hydropower stations blocking their migratory routes, parasites, pesticides and pollution poisoning water and killing their prey, and even noisy shipping which is thought to reduce their ability to avoid predators. Once a staple fare for creatures such as otters and herons, as eel numbers diminish river predators turn to fish for the bulk of their diets. Sadly, this once prolific source of food for so many species, including humans, has been unable to compete in an over-peopled world. Eels could disappear in a few years.

I was pleased to see this one and hoped he would make a hasty meal of any crayfish he encountered. Eels are great predators and powerful enough to tackle quite large crayfish; another valuable role they fulfil in a river. And perhaps, one day, he would make the return journey across the ocean. Eels can reach a great age, there are stories of them living over a hundred years in captivity but, mysteriously, they never breed until they get back to the Sargasso Sea.

With an idea to cast further up, I stood and edged out into the tail of the pool, but was distracted for a moment by some shouting. A man with a maroon pullover stretched over an ample gut marched slowly across the field, his back braced against the weight he carried in front. At every step he bawled at two terriers who pottered about unconcerned, clearly accustomed to the incessant noise. Relieved to find that my attention was not required I turned back to the pool and saw, just below my rod and less than two thirds of its seven foot length away from me, three grayling holding station in the current. I held my breath.

Of course, grayling were out of season and I didn't really want to catch them, in fact it would have been impossible to cast to them from that position anyway and I wondered whether they knew that when a pool is being fished the safest place is close to the fisherman's waders, but I didn't want to alarm them as they would have disturbed the rest of the pool.

After waiting motionless for what seemed hours but was really only a few minutes, my patience exhausted, I cast up the pool again with one eye on my fly and the other on the fish at my feet. The grayling didn't move. I thought the action of my rod directly above them would be sure to send them darting for cover but they seemed oblivious to my presence. If only fish could be so relaxed when I'm trying to catch them; but perhaps they know the difference.

My fly drifted back down the pool towards me and I saw both dry fly and nymph pass the grayling with no response, so I lifted my rod to cast again and as the fly cleared the surface felt a sharp tug on the nymph. One of them must have followed it and just as he took I had snatched it out of his mouth. Never mind, I was not really trying to catch them (but any fish would be nice).

I moved on up the pool, casting a few times, taking one or two paces forwards, casting again, trying all the interesting looking places, beside weed clumps, in the bubble line, under the far bank. Near the top of the pool I changed to a side cast to avoid a willow reaching overhead from the right bank behind me. A coppiced alder clung to the far bank and I cast towards its red roots.

Suddenly it happened. Close to the roots the fly was snapped up; too fast to think, my strike happened automatically and I connected with a chunky body of vibrant, watery life. He zipped about in ever shorter dashes and darts as I pulled him close, twanged the net over my shoulder on its elastic lanyard and scooped him in. A glorious trout – pewter and silver, spotted with jet and dotted with tiny rubies. Even in the net he thrashed about and because he was the first of the season, although a notable trout at any time of year, I took a photograph. Then I held the fly and gave it a brisk shake to let him wriggle off back to the whispering stream.

There was a huge smile on my face and in my heart as this little fish reassured me that spring was here at last, fly life would hatch, fish would rise (and I might possibly be able to catch some of them) and the river was awakening from its long winter torpor. A frog in the rushes repeated a raspy piping call, birdsong swelled from the woods steeping up on either side of the little meadow and as the late sun, netted in filigree branches, sank towards Pixton Hill it glinted off the surface of the stream highlighting every swirl and eddy, silver on the riffles, pewter in the glides, with jet black shadow on the deep pool under the bank.

CHAPTER 23

Riverfly

Bury Bridge spans the River Haddeo in two round and two pointed arches where little spleenwort ferns with fine black stems find a hold in lime mortar within the stonework. The hump-backed, medieval pack-horse bridge is too narrow for most traffic but there is a ford alongside it and there Roger unpacked containers, nets and various such equipment from the back of his van.

Rivers are more than simply an elemental fusion of energy, water and rock – within this dynamic system they seethe with life. As well as fish there are worms and leeches, shrimps and snails, spiders and beetles and millions of animals too small to see without a microscope. Flies fluttering over a summer stream are only the short-lived reproductive forms of creatures who spend most of the year underwater. Burrowing into silt, waving through weed, clinging to rock or nestling between stones, tiny beings shelter from the tearing current and we seldom notice them but if we take the trouble to look the information they can give us is immensely valuable.

The Anglers' Riverfly Monitoring Initiative is organised by a group of scientists, conservationists and anglers with the aim of watching over the health of rivers through surveying populations of aquatic invertebrates. Volunteers are trained and equipped to carry out a simple monitoring exercise on their local rivers and the results provide a valuable picture of the health of our watercourses.

Roger held a long handled net close to the riverbed, just downstream of his wader boots, and shuffled through the pebbles while I timed him. His trundling feet released debris to be washed into the fine-meshed net and when he finally sloshed out of the river several double handfuls of dark gravelly sludge had been collected. This was tipped into a white plastic tray where it squirmed with life. We peered into the shallow tray, Roger's grey forelock flopping over his eyes, and examined the dozens of different creatures wriggling around. I wondered how I should ever learn to identify them all.

"You don't need to," Roger reassured me. He explained that we were looking for just four main types of invertebrate: the larvae of up-winged flies such as mayflies which all have three tails; stonefly larvae with two tails; caddis fly larvae; and freshwater shrimps.

"These are important groups to monitor because they are all very sensitive to pollution, so they act as indicators of water quality."

"So if there are plenty of these the river should be clean?"

"That's right. We check the same sites regularly and if numbers suddenly fall we know there's a problem."

We sorted the little creatures into groups in a segmented container, sweeping them into a teaspoon with a paintbrush or sucking them up with a pipette as they scuttled around the tray. (This part of the exercise appealed to my childish sense of fun.) We found twenty seven caddis, sixty or so olives and stone clingers, six stone flies and a mayfly. I carried the tray into shallow water, slopped some around to wash it out and returned everything as carefully as possible to the stream where it belonged.

Rivers are heartbreakingly vulnerable to pollution. We have a lifestyle dependent upon so many unnatural substances – fuels, fire retardants, wood treatments, the list is endless before we even consider chemicals deliberately intended to be poisonous like pesticides for killing fleas, woodworm, slugs, wasps and the rest. We use these noxious concoctions with little thought for where they will go, what harm they may do, after we have released them into the world. Dogs regularly have insecticide applied to their coats and are then encouraged to play in the river. People slather themselves in sunscreen and then swim in the river. Everything spilled on a road or poured into a ditch, either accidentally or deliberately, ends up in the river. Everything we wash down a drain or flush down a toilet heads for the river. We use rivers as drains to flush the filth of humanity into the sea and our disdain for these precious environments is shocking. Whilst most people are thoughtful in their actions, some are not, and knowing that pollution is being monitored and is traceable encourages a great deal more care.

Aquatic invertebrates are useful indicators of water quality because of their sensitivity to pollution. If some noxious substance is spilled into a river, the current washes it away fairly quickly so chemical analysis of the water is unhelpful in identifying its point of origin. However, invertebrates downstream from the source of contamination can take months or years to recover, pointing, even in death, an indisputable finger of blame.

The next site we visited was the shallow riffle just below Bracken Bank Pool, lower down the Haddeo. This time it was my turn to shuffle about in the river holding the net to collect another tray load of tiny river creatures. Then we sat comfortably in the sun on the grassy rim of the pool, our feet dangling in the water and the tray of invertebrates between us. We began catching and sorting them to the rhythmic cheeping of pheasant poults picking their way between nettles and Himalayan balsam on the opposite bank.

In the pool beside us a fish rose. The sound lifted my eyes from the tray and as my focus extended into the golden green depths I could see a fish holding station beside a pale rock. There was another about a foot or so behind it. Gently swaying in the current, they hung about mid depth in the water and were clearly taking food from the surface. Both fish came up to investigate drifting debris from time to time, occasionally accelerating into a quick snatch, but what they were taking I could not see. After a few minutes the splash of a heavy rise revealed the presence of a larger fish near the head of the pool and, staring past the rolling stream of light playing over the faceted surface, I saw two more of goodish size.

Suddenly, I remembered what I was supposed to be doing and apologised for my distraction. "Oh, sorry, Roger. I got quite carried away watching those fish."

But I needn't have worried – Roger was watching them too. The two fish nearest the tail of the pool were within a few feet of us yet appeared quite unconcerned by our presence, continuing to take some unidentifiable morsels from the provisioning current.

We completed our invertebrate count, finding thirty or so olives, thirty fat-bodied stone clingers, nineteen caddis, three stoneflies, two mayflies and two freshwater shrimps. The equipment gathered together, we trudged back across the field and packed up the van. Then, taking off his waders, Roger kindly offered to close the gate behind me.

"Oh, thank you, but please don't worry," I said. "I might not leave just yet."

As he drove away I made a quick phone call to establish that no one else was fishing the Haddeo today and the beat was all mine if I wanted it. I did.

In the back of my car I found a seven foot rod and was soon back at Bracken Bank Pool where fish were still rising but however hard I stared I could not make out what they were taking. It was tiny though, so I offered a size sixteen Pale Watery but this was declined. On two occasions I saw fish come to examine it and turn away. So, to alternate a light coloured fly with a dark, I tried a similar sized Black Smut, just a tiny pinch of mole fur wound onto the hook shank with a scant wisp of duck feather for the suggestion of a tail.

A pile of brash awaited a bonfire in the field behind me so I kept the line high on the back cast to avoid snaggling and sent the little Smut towards the top of the pool where I could now see only one of the two fish who had been there earlier. The fly landed quite nicely a few inches in front of the fish but he ignored it as it slowly drifted over his nose and passed him by a foot, two feet, three feet. Sploop!

Perhaps the fish had thought better of declining a snack and turned or perhaps I had hooked the second fish I'd lost sight of but suddenly a fish was on – a decent sized fish, bending my rod over the pool. He leaped a couple of times in energetic resistance, flashing in the sunlight, splashing vigorously, sending ripples across the river and finally submitted to my net. He was a hefty handful, spotted as a cheetah, and I took a moment to admire him before letting him spin from my fingers back to the pool with a fishy flourish.

The Black Smut was rather wet and bedraggled after its adventure so I dried it off in a tissue, fluffed it up a bit and administered a dusting of desiccant powder to revive it. Despite the drama the pool had just witnessed, calm was quickly restored and fish resumed their rising. So I cast the little Smut across the pool once more and fanned a series of casts upstream but received no further response. A couple more flies were tried with no greater success and then, at last, I managed to watch a fish feeding close enough to see what he was taking; they were small, nondescript beige-coloured flies that fluttered and trembled on the surface. I didn't know their name but looked for a fly pattern to imitate their general colour and proportions. A classic Deer Hair Sedge seemed the closest match. My smallest one, having seen some past action, looked somewhat tatty but had proved its worth more than once so I tied it on.

At the first cast, which was towards the centre of the pool, the fly wobbled on the current for a second and disappeared. I lifted the rod instinctively without considering (because there wasn't time to consider) whether the disappearance was due to being tumbled in the current or whether it may have been a sip from an unseen fish.

It was a fish!

He dived deep and the taut line cut circles through the surface of the pool as he swam strong loops before coming to my waiting net. Another splendid trout as plump as the first but coloured quite differently, finely freckled and distinctively silvered.

These trout were both in fine condition and endorsed the results of our Riverfly survey; they had clearly found an abundance of invertebrate food and a good living in this nourishing, beneficent stream.

CHAPTER 24

A Summer Afternoon

Flowers of red and white clover, purple self heal, yellow rattle and cat's ear filled the hay meadow with colour, mingling with grasses – bents and fescues, sweet vernal grass, crested dog's tail – old fashioned grasses with the gracious manners to accommodate wildflowers in their midst. It was high summer and yellow rattle was just forming the rattling seed pods it is named for. There was a scattering of grasshoppers, bees, butterflies and small, pale moths from my footsteps.

I walked carefully around the edge of the hay meadow, following hedge and riverbank, trying to trample as little as possible the grass that would be needed for sheep-feed in winter. Where bracken creeps out from the bank, at the junction of the Haddeo with the River Exe, a venerable oak tree extends his roots along the banks of both rivers, introducing the two waters with a handshake, and here I stepped down the riverbank into the stream; a place where the current whispers over water-worn pebbles of sepia, sienna, ochre, umber and terracotta punctuated with an occasional rough, white quartz, flickered with sunlight, netted with shadows.

I cast a pale Deer Hair Sedge fly upstream and watched it bob back towards me on the current, sitting up on the surface like an insect carried on the meniscus, and as it came I gathered in spare line to keep in touch with the fly. Branches of alder, oak and ash prevent overhead casts in most places so it usually has to be a side cast for the Haddeo. The current swirls deeply around fibrous red alder roots in a pool where there is always a fish but my first cast produced nothing. So I cast again, a little further to the right each time, fanning across the pool and it was in the shallower water towards the pebbly beach on the other side that I finally got a rise. He was small but vibrant, leaping on the end of my line with fizzing energy and when I unhooked him he whizzed off at speed.

So I fished on up the river and twice had to untangle the line from hemlock water dropwort leaning over the stream and then missed a couple of rises through being too slow, but in the pool below the bridge I caught two. Although not large they were exceptionally beautiful, dark fish, bronze flanked with chocolate coloured backs and cherry spots.

Such stunning fish had me fumbling for the camera to try to capture them again in photographs before releasing them. I made a poor job of the first one, badly arranged and out of focus, and then with the second fish the camera fell into the river. I grabbed it hastily and wiped it off with a handkerchief hoping it hadn't suffered too much damage. I am always in a hurry to release fish, anxious not to cause them harm, and this was the priority. My photographic ineptitude might have been depressing but remembering the three beautiful trout I had just caught restored my confidence so I relaxed, forgot about photographs and simply enjoyed being with the river.

The Deer Hair Sedge was understandably looking a little tired after all its adventures, so I cut it off and selected a French partridge hackle mayfly. I had seen one or two mayfly dipping into the stream. Not many, but perhaps just enough to sharpen a trout's appetite.

I waded under the old ivy-veiled stone bridge where dippers nest on the ledge. Within the echoing archway the river's voice becomes hollow, deeper, more emphatic and the stonework feels flaky and crusty. Stalactites like pale roots grow where water leaches through the lime mortar and cobwebs lace between them, woven by the spiders whose clutches of eggs are secreted in crevices in the stonework, safely wrapped in tiny cotton-wool balls.

Above the bridge a fish rose to my fly but I was too slow and missed him, the momentum of my strike sending the line instead into bushes opposite. Had I not already caught three fish I should have found this vexing but now, calm and unperturbed, I sat on the white rock where otters always mark to sort it all out. Spraint on the rock smelled musky-sweet, and I enjoyed an otter's eye view of the river for a while.

Then I worked my way up the stream between banks sweet with honeysuckle and wild white roses and I hooked another fish that came off just before I could bring him to hand, but grey wagtails tapped their metronome tails and mayflies danced above the stream and I was still smiling – it didn't matter. And like a flash of summer sky, a kingfisher came zipping down the river, racing the current, swerving around the bend, gone in a whistle.

Just before a big bend a fallen tree blocks the way so I climbed out of the river into the field and walked around the obstruction to Bracken Bank Pool. The bank there is thick with bracken and hemlock water dropwort and I tried to make use of this cover to slip down the bank and sit on a log at the edge of the water. Time for a piece of chocolate while I watched the pool.

There was a fish rising on my right under a young withy bush, another higher up the pool close to the bank, one in midstream. There were fish everywhere, but this pool is difficult to fish because the water is calm, clear and well lit. It calls for subtlety, subversion even. You have to hide.

I cast short to begin with to avoid spooking fish by casting over them. The tall growth on the bank behind me meant the line must be kept high on the back cast and it must be put down softly without a splash on the glassy surface of the pool. The first few casts produced nothing. I fanned out towards the withy. Nothing. A little further up the pool and as the fly floated slowly towards me a fish rose, actually leapt clear of the water right beside it, but didn't take. In the slow, clear water he must have seen the leader in the surface or recognised the fly for an artifice and become alarmed. It wasn't a very big fish but he may have disturbed the rest of the pool.

I sat on the log again and watched a while longer. A slow procession of bubbles across the dark pool brought with them the occasional leaf, a few rose petals, and there must have been insects too for in a little while there was another rise. It wasn't many minutes before the fish below the bush rose again, leaving concentric circles like a target inviting my aim on the smooth surface of the water. I couldn't see what they were taking but saw no reason why they would refuse a mayfly if it was offered.

The difficulty was how to put the fly into the right spot without either disturbing the pool or being seen by the fish. I had to avoid bracken and tall weeds on the bank as well as trees on my left while somehow curving the line around the bush to put the fly softly into the bubble line just beyond. It was a tricky cast and the wind was gusting unhelpfully.

After watching a few more rises I could delay the moment no longer. Half standing, half crouching in the cover of weed, I crept into the edge of the pool, lifted the rod as high as I could reach above my shoulder and aimed for a spot alongside the withy. It didn't work. A gust of wind took the line into the stems and a quick backwards flick failed to release it, only embedding the fly ever more firmly in the twigs. There was no way it would loosen its hold and wading out into the pool would put down every fish. I pulled at the line hopelessly.

With my rod held high above weed I shuffled backwards up the bank, not daring to stand until a safe distance from the water, then walked around the bend to where to the withy was rooted in the bank. It was not large but several whippy stems hung out over the pool, my fly was in one of them and the line wrapped around others in a twangy tangle. The supple stems were not strong enough to lean on but somehow I pulled them in to the bank without snapping the leader, did not quite over-balance and fall in the river and managed to retrieve my fly. I crept back to the log below the bank and prepared to try again. When my line was reorganised I edged into the pool behind the weed, lifted my rod above it and cast high. This time the fly landed in the river. It fell into the bubble line close to the withy bush and trembled a little as the current brought it towards me but my heart began to sink as it passed the spot where the fish had been without eliciting a reaction. He wasn't taking this fly.

SPLOOSH!

Suddenly, at a tremendous splash, I lifted the rod in disbelief and connected with something hefty. He set off around the pool with determination and I quickly wound up slack line to control him on the reel. Slowly I wound him in and as he came closer the flash of a silver flank turned in the depths. This was a good fish. As he was drawn towards my extended net I wondered whether he would fit into it. Still thrashing wildly, his gleaming body folded almost double as he gathered himself for the next leap, I scooped him in.

A magnificent trout, lithe and muscly, his belly white gold, his flank silver, the top of his back the same rich dark browns as the pebbled riverbed yet at the same time brilliantly shining. Thickly mottled with night-black spots, each one haloed in pearly moonlight, he was a king amongst fish. I held him in the net, keeping him in the water to admire him and to remove the hook from his cavernous mouth and took out my camera.

Here, at last, was a fish worth photographing, but the camera had not recovered from its dip in the river and refused to work. Ah well, I should not need a picture to remember this fish. He was almost the length of the net from the bowed top to the handle and from later calculations with a ruler I believe he measured fourteen and a half inches from nose to tail. As he slipped away into the welcoming current with unhurried majesty I gave thanks to the little river for the privilege of making his acquaintance.

CHAPTER 25

How to Wash a River

"What we are going to do . . ." Alistair began, wading out into mid-stream with an iron bar, "is firstly to loosen a patch of gravel." He demonstrated to the assembled working-party how to stab the bar down into the riverbed, digging and levering it about to release stones from the sediment settled between them cementing it all together. It appeared quite solid and hard to break up but already dirty clouds of mud billowed downstream from his bar.

After a few minutes of this work Alistair, tall and quietly authoritative, returned to the bank to swap his iron bar for a garden leaf-blower. With a tug on the cord, he started up the little two-stroke engine and carried the puttering machine out to the middle of the river. "Once it's loose we can blow it clean." We saw how the long nozzle must be dug into the broken sub-strate, revving the accelerator to blast air into the loosened pebbles, churning them around in an eruption of white water like a washing machine escaped from its drum. When a patch of around a yard across had been cleaned to his satisfaction, Alistair marked a number one on a yellow painted stake and hammered it into the adjacent bank. One of the team had a phone app that produced a ten figure grid reference for the site which was noted on a clipboard.

"This can be your job." I was passed the marker pen, mallet and clipboard, which gave me a worryingly official appearance. The willing assembly of volunteers from Dulverton Angling Association were organised into teams of two, and one of each wader-clad pair was issued with an iron bar, the other with a leaf-blower.

So we set off along the River Haddeo, working downstream, to clean around twenty strategically sited patches with the aim of creating areas of silt free gravel because this is what salmon need to find for spawning. The treated patches of gravel stood out, clean and light coloured, against the darkly dirty riverbed around them but to be sure of finding them again I banged in a yellow marker stake beside each one.

It is called 'gravel' but tends rather towards the coarser end of that description, being smallish stones of between two and four inches across amongst which salmon find ideal conditions to secrete their eggs. The stone pieces must not be so small that they too readily become clogged with silt but small enough and free enough to be moved by fish when they come to cut their redds, hollow excavations in the gravel where they will spawn.

Their spherical orange eggs will lodge amongst loose stones which save them from being swept away in the brisk current whilst allowing oxygen rich water to constantly bubble through. Silt and mud smother fish eggs causing them to fail due to deoxygenation.

We hoped to provide these patches of clean gravel in areas of the river where spawning salmon would naturally seek them. The requirement for a silt-free substrate means that slow bends, deep places and other areas of fine gravel, sand and mud are avoided. Fast water in a riffle is unsuitable because eggs would be washed away before they could be fertilised and covered over. The favourite position is at the tail of a pool, especially where gravel is ramped up, supporting the pool, and water filters through pebbles as it accelerates into a riffle. In places like this the current continually washes out silt, keeping gravel clean and loose and oxygenating the eggs. Of course, washing fine parti-cles out of the riverbed does mean a loss of invertebrates living there so we avoided the river margins, which are especially rich in invertebrate life, and restricted our cleaning to small patches of around a square yard each. The carefully considered siting of these patches would be the key to success.

Like all Exmoor streams, the Haddeo is a freestone river. These rivers descend from hills where steep gradients give veloc-ity to their currents, cutting into the land, carving away pieces of rock which fall into their courses to create loose stony beds. It is the nature of such rivers to rise and fall quickly in response to rainfall and in times of spate the power of their water is immense. The action of water moving stone against stone abrades sharper edges, rounding them into smooth pebbles to roll ever more freely with the journeying stream. Particles are moved and dropped according to the velocity of the current – larger stones fall to the bottom to be moved only in the strongest spates while smaller pebbles, gravel, sand and silt are continuously shuffled downstream. Gravels and sands are dropped where the current loses impetus, such as on the inside of a bend, fine particles of clay are carried furthest in suspen-sion, sometimes for miles, and only settle out of the water where it almost stills, in deep quiet pools. So currents sort sub-strate into different zones, arranging the varied formation of the river. On the Haddeo, however, this natural process has been interrupted by the dam built across the valley to impound Wimbleball reservoir.

Years ago, before the reservoir was built, the River Haddeo was an important spawning ground for salmon but the dam has amputated its upper reaches and changed the nature of the river below, which can sometimes get badly silted up. The reser-voir stores water for domestic supply in Tiverton, Exeter and the surrounding area which is taken from the River Exe, water being released from the reservoir to compensate in times of low flow and impounded for storage when rivers are high.

So the Haddeo experiences flow levels opposite to those in the River Exe and neighbouring rivers – higher in dry weather and lower in wet. This means that when other rivers are in spate salmon migrating upstream to spawn will unexpectedly meet low water here, and when fry emerge in summer water may be high and the current strong. It was in recognition of this anomaly that the River Haddeo was being treated to special care and attention.

It was not easy to use machinery whilst slithering about on slippery pebbles, buffeted by a strong current, and everyone got wet. One of the leaf-blowers kept stalling. The end of its nozzle was slightly flattened, increasing the velocity of air it expelled, which might be handy in a garden but underwater the pressure was just too much for the little motor to cope with. So the narrowed section was hacked off with a sturdy pocket knife, leaving the tube as an unchoked open cylinder, which solved the problem at once and the machine revved away happily for the rest of the morning.

After a few hours' work we stopped for a break and Alistair produced a crate of beer which was received with groans of relief. It was tough work and everyone was glad to sit on the riverbank and rest. Beer and bags of crisps were passed around, I ate chocolate and we watched a hatch of small flies above the river. One of the gravel washers, Dil, snapped out a big arm to snatch one deftly from the air and held the tiny insect gently in large hands.

"It's a blue winged olive."

"There are so many! Isn't it rather late in the year for those?"

Clearly it wasn't as they fluttered up from the water in clouds. Fish began to rise. There were only three days left of the season and Alistair must have seen the look on our faces as he dismissed most of us, insisting he could do the last site he had in mind with just one helper.

Dil and I went fishing.

* * *

A grey, damp morning in the third week of November, the Haddeo valley hung with veils of mist obscuring the tops of the wooded hillsides. A bewhiskered face below a crumpled tweed fishing hat peered out of a four wheel drive vehicle.

"Morning, Fred!" I called.

"Good morning, Michelle. A bit of a wet morning, but the river's not too high, not too coloured."

"No, the water's fine," I agreed.

We walked along the riverbank and I pointed out the patches of gravel we had worked so hard to clean a couple of months earlier. "This is the spot where we started gravel washing, just along here."

I showed Fred the yellow stakes we had put in to mark cleaned patches. Our task that morning was to revisit them and try to determine whether any had been used by fish. It would be exciting to find a redd, as I had never seen one, and even better to see a salmon. I knew they spawned in this river because I had sometimes caught little salmon parr when fishing for trout.

"Have you seen a redd before?" I asked hopefully.

"Not really," Fred admitted.

Salmon on the River Exe reached a sorry state in the mid-nineteenth century from the cumulative effects of weirs, pollution and over exploitation. They were rescued from the brink of disaster by legislation to introduce close seasons, prohibit taking of young, spawning and 'unclean' fish, banning certain unfair methods of fish destruction and imposing powers to install fish passes where they were needed. A dramatic recovery occurred just in time for fishermen to take advantage of superb water conditions which led to a record catch of some four thousand fish in 1897. Then, in the early 1970s disaster unfolded again with an outbreak of Ulcerative Dermal Necrosis, a potentially fatal skin condition from which the population took several years to recover.

Now climate change presents fish with new challenges; it is

believed that warmer temperatures during spawning might inhibit the production and viability of eggs and that cold temperatures at emergence could reduce the availability of aquatic invertebrates at that vital time, causing hunger or even starvation for emerging trout and salmon fry. When they reach the sea, migratory trout and salmon find less food there too, probably because sea water is warming. Older fishermen have told me how grilse, salmon returning after one year at sea, used regularly to weigh around five to seven pounds. Now they weigh three.

The fortunes of Atlantic salmon have always fluctuated erratically, yet the truly worrying consideration is the wider view; global populations have fallen from around eight to ten million in the 1970s to a sorry three to four million today. Catch numbers on the River Exe from the last seventy years show an irregular but undeniable decline to less than a fifth. Migratory fish today face so many threats to their survival; weirs and hydro-electric installations presenting barriers to both spawning fish migrating upstream and smolts migrating down, the by-catch of commercial fisheries at sea and an increase in predation. So, on this river which has been damaged in rather a major way for human convenience, any extra care we can offer is little enough recompense.

Fred and I searched the stream bed, finding the yellow stakes and checking all the sites where gravel had been cleaned and a few other likely looking spots as well. I was a little disappointed at how thoroughly indistinguishable the cleaned patches had become, with the same darkened complexion as the rest of the riverbed, and hoped the dirtying was only on the surface. I wondered whether we would recognise a redd if we found one but as we scanned the river, examining every depression amongst tumbled rocks and pebbles below the shattered surface of the water, I was far from sure. Nevertheless, we spent an interesting morning in the deep Haddeo valley. Squirrels skipped across the track, a heron lifted off the river in angular splendour and a group of hinds threaded their way through the mist between trees on the hillside above us.

We found nothing we could confidently call a redd that morning, nor the following week when we repeated the exercise.

It was the first week of December when we visited the valley for the third time and winter was mouldering away the autumn, turning the sodden woodland floor dark red. A dipper sang from a mid-stream rock, stitching silvery chains of song through the white noise of white water.

At the lowest spot we checked, just below Bracken Bank Pool, the current is divided by an old alder stump and the slack water between the two streams has gathered a raised bar of gravel and sticks, reinforcing the division with the embryonic beginnings of an island. Fred and I scanned the river from the left bank above the main current and, in the smaller stream on the far side of the bar, we could see a little bubble of white water that was not quite the same as all the other bubbles of white water tumbling over rocks throughout the length of the river. It was difficult to say why, but this was different and we waded across to have a closer look.

At the head of the riffle we found a pit in the riverbed about nine inches deep, twice the depth of water on either side and, in contrast with brownish pebbles around it, the lighter cleaner stones at the bottom were purplish red, pale grey, dark slate with a few small white flecks of quartz. At the lower end of this hole a small heap of stones blotted with oak and hazel leaves stood raised in the stream and it was over this that water was bubbling.

"Ah!" Fred exclaimed. "That looks interesting."

"Oh yes, this does look right, doesn't it!"

We waded in to have a closer look, taking care not to step on the disturbed area. The excavation was far more obvious than we had expected and we were both quite certain we had found a freshly cut redd.

I imagined silver salmon, born here in this stream, who had lived for maybe three years in the North Atlantic Ocean on a diet of sand eels, herring and sprats which enabled them to grow larger and stronger than they ever could in a river, now returning to the place of their birth. And what drew them back? The moon, the tides, some quality of the light, perhaps? We humans understand so little of the world.

There were hungry seals, sharks and killer wales to avoid, massive trawler nets and foul spills of oil and diesel. It was a dangerous journey but somehow they reached the estuary where surging tides met the brown waters of the River Exe somewhere between Exmouth and Dawlish, and there they waited for rain to swell the river into spate, to carry down the scent of woods and moors, the smell of Exmoor, to draw them home.

When the spate came, they went. Powering up some fifty miles of the River Exe against the current, flinging themselves forward, heedless of injury, leaping every one of the almost impassable weirs, sometimes swimming up a sheer wall of water, often falling back and leaping again, never troubling to eat, following the scent of the soil, of mouldering bracken and oak leaves, of pheasants, sheep and deer; a rich chord of scent remembered from the earliest days of their lives, just as I remember scents of places from my childhood – the smell of school (plasticine, crayons and boiled cabbage) and of my grandparents' farm with the big barn that smelled of grain and cobwebs and the distinctive smells of the fowls' house, shippens, stables, and the cosy farmhouse with its buttery fragrance of scalding milk to make clotted cream. The unregarded yet unforgettable scents of home.

By the time they reached the Haddeo the salmon were almost exhausted. And here, in this shallow backwater, on this rubble of pebbles, a hen fish cut her redd. She turned on to her side, undulated her body with heaving ripples of effort and by flapping her broad tail caused sufficient turbulence to lift stones into the current which rolled them downstream. In this way she excavated a pit and when it was of sufficient size she lay in it, arched her body, threw back her head with mouth stretched open and expelled her orange eggs. The cock fish, trembling beside her, could hold his milt no longer and, mouth gaping as wide as hers, he let it gush over them. At once, the hen fish moved forwards dislodging stones just upstream to cover the precious fertilised eggs and scooped a second pit into which she released more eggs and the cock fish more milt, and she covered them with stones as before. The pit we discovered would have been the last and uppermost in the chain. The fish may have done this two or three times before falling away as spent kelts, their silver scales rusted dark and the purpose of their lives ful-filled. Their eggs secreted within the stones below were the seed of the next generation, completing the endless cycle, perpetu-ating the eternity of the life-giving stream.

The River Exe

CHAPTER 26

Moor of Streams

—

Gentle hands of the wind tousle sedges and moor grass on top of Dure Down, a high boggy land where drainings from the hill seep into a chamber between slate slabs set squarely into the earth. Peaty water emerges from this rough casket to run over a flat stone inscribed with the words 'Exe Head', marking the significance of this unremarkable trickle. The newborn stream crosses a track and sets off northwards where the sea lies no more than five miles away but quickly swings right handed, turning inland to gurgle under Blackpitts Bridge and chuckle down the combe between Prayway Meads and Great Ashcome heading south east to begin its long journey towards Exmouth, some sixty miles away on the south coast of Devon.

The name 'Exe' comes from 'Isca', the old Brittonic and imitative word for running water and particularly for streams abounding in fish, so, Exmoor which takes its name from the river, means 'moor of streams'. Conversely the River Exe is the river of the moor, carrying with it traces of soil, the stain of peat, the colour and scent of the land even to the far-off city of Exeter, like the moor-born folk whose speech never loses the distinguishing accents of the land where they were raised.

The River Exe runs between steep hills, through deep valleys it has carved for itself over aeons of its passing. It runs below hill farms, Warren, Westermill, Wellshead and is joined by many little streams whose waters come chattering down the combes; from Rams Combe and Rat Combe, Sparkham Water, Allcombe Water, Edgcott Water and many others whose names I have forgotten, or never knew or perhaps were never named. With every contributing rivulet the stream grows in strength and significance and the first village it passes through, Exford, is named for the ancient crossing of river and road; an important place from the days before bridges were built. Twisting onwards through farmland and woodland, the Larcombe Brook, the Winn Brook and the River Quarme add their forces to the ever increasing river. Oak, ash, sycamore and alder stand on the banks to watch it pass and dippers and kingfishers follow its course. In slow flows the riverbed appears a uniform caramel colour but when rinsed by heavy rains the spate-scoured stones are the earthy pastel tones of sage and sand, verdigris and peach, mulberry, smoke and ashes of violets.

The Dulverton Angling Association offers access to some interestingly varied stretches of water and one of my favourite beats is Hollam. The river here is known as the Little Exe, distinguishing it from the mighty river it becomes below The Meeting of the Waters where it is joined by the greater River Barle.

Between precipitous woodlands on either side where spinning, piping calls of peregrines lift over the valley, this beat lies close to the road, yet is secluded by trees with the sound of traffic obscured in the constant voice of the river. As it is so close to home I often pop down for a couple of hours after work, escaping professional concerns to spend time with the Exe. Then, of course, time evaporates and I forget that any such measure of life exists, aware only of the river, until gathering dusk obscures my fly, drags my eyes reluctantly from the stream and reminds me to go home. Hours spent in company with the river are always enriching and life affirming; relaxing in times of stress, reviving at times of staleness, cheering on days of sadness and always brightening as reflected sunlight sparkles from the shimmering surface. And like the best of companions, the river often makes me laugh and sometimes laughs at me.

On the evening of a warm day drifted over by flossy clouds a few mayfly danced over the stream. These creatures, who live for a year or more in mud and silt at the bottom of a river and transform into glistening adult flies for just one day, sometimes two, sometimes only hours, are a curious source of wonder. The nymphs living in mud can have no concept of flight yet when it is their time, questingly, they crawl out of water into the unfamiliar element of air. Do adult flies, fluttering over the stream, remember living in its depths? If they do, the new miracle of sunlit flight must be astonishingly elating. And if they do not, if their one day with wings is all the life of which they are conscious, what a glorious life it must be – if all they know is one summer day on a river.

Anyway, when there are mayfly over the stream, even I know enough to try fishing an imitation of one and, indeed, an abstract copy tied with a French partridge feather proved most acceptable and attracted some rises; but either the fish didn't take or my strike was too slow and nothing was caught. However, always hopeful, I fished my way up the river undeterred until I reached the ruins of a broken weir.

Fast water cascaded around my legs as I stood below the shattered masonry and cast into the line of bubbles streaming towards me over deep, dark water held within the structure's remains. The fly had drifted halfway back when it was devoured in a hefty gulp and I lifted into a sizeable fish. He dashed towards me and I grabbed in line fast in an effort to maintain contact but the fish got in amongst the rocks and rubble of the tumbled weir and I feared I might lose him there. By some good luck he didn't come off and I crumpled onto a rock maintaining tension with my rod hand whilst reaching into the water with my left, following the line under the ledge, down through invisible, stone-roofed depths until I felt fish. I drew out a chunky handful of trout and admired his sturdy build, his bronze and ruby splendour as I relieved him of the hook, gave him a kiss and returned him to the reviving current.

I fished on where the river becomes rough and rocky and progress is clambering slow, where white water tumbles between small pools and each pocket of sheltered water holds a little trout. A few more rises were missed; they were tiny and quick and too subtle for me. Then, between high wooded banks enclosing the river, I crept forward to crouch behind a convenient boulder from where I could cast unseen into a little pool ahead.

As I made the cast, at the periphery of my consciousness an awareness of movement amongst bushes on the bank tapped at my mind, demanding attention, but my concentration was focussed on line and fly and I couldn't lift my eyes from the river until I had fished it in, although on this occasion there was no fish. When I finally looked up I saw antlers.

Three pairs of antlers were nodding on the riverbank – no, there were four. My view was partly obscured by bushes and vegetation so I could not see the bodies of the stags, just their half-formed summer antlers, softly encased in velvet. They were all young stags, probably two and three years old, wandering along the riverside path and in and out of the woods beyond.

I sat quietly on a nearby rock, which was downwind of them, and although quite close the stags didn't notice me but continued to browse along between woodland and riverbank. I ate some chocolate, listened to the sharp song of a wren cutting cleanly through the noise of rushing waters and watched the rounded, fuzzy tines of their antlers metronoming as they plucked leaves from springy twigs and occasionally shook with the irritation of flies.

After a while they moved beyond my sight. How long had I been watching them? It might have been five minutes or twenty, I had no idea, but when I could no longer see them my attention was drawn back to fish. I made a few more casts in the pool before me but there was no response so climbed over rocks to the river's edge where I could more easily move upstream to the next pool.

On a mossy stone between fast runs lay the sad but glorious remains of a damselfly. Three teardrop shaped wings glowed with deep, vibrant colour; a rich petrel blue, a royal green; colour too luminous to read. Probably the insect had been an important meal for a bird, maybe the wren or perhaps a dipper. Like mayflies, damselflies spend most of their lives as nymphs amongst underwater weed, only emerging to transform into the bright fluttering-winged creatures we know for mating and egg laying. Perhaps that purpose had been fulfilled. I carefully put the three teardrops into my fly tin and carried on fishing, wanting to catch just one more fish so that the humiliation of the many who had so easily eluded me did not shadow the evening.

I reached the bank and suddenly a sycamore bush beside me exploded, throwing up its leaves like hands in shock, making my heart jolt briefly as a heavy body crashed through rattling branches and frantic hooves scrabbled and galloped away. The stag must have been even more surprised than I was.

I did catch another fish, close to the footbridge where I finished; another weighty trout of a decent size, perhaps eight or nine inches, I am so bad at guessing measurements. Anyway, he was splendid and as I returned him to the cool stream I felt grateful to the forgiving river; although I had only caught two fish they were both considerably larger than average for that stretch of the Exe and the stags had been fun so there was a genuine smile on my lips as I ambled back down the valley to go home.

In the morning, remembering the damselfly wings, I opened my fly box to admire them again but found they had turned black. All that dynamic, zinging colour had fled, perhaps rejoined with the spirit of the damselfly – a creature of both water and air living in colour too intense and heavenly to last long in this world, perhaps ephemeral as a rainbow against glowering cloud or as reflections on water, perhaps returned home to the weed and pebbles of the endless current.

CHAPTER 27

Old Woman's

It was a dull, damp July morning, not too hot, not too windy, and promised to be an ideal day for fishing. I met Josh sitting in his red pick-up beside the River Exe and as we walked along the beat he told me about all the best holding places for fish, describing the character of every pool, run and riffle. Enthusiasm sparkled from his dark eyes as he remembered fish from every part of the river and it quickly became clear that the fish he was passionate about were salmon. That was great for me, as his lack of interest in trout meant he was quite happy for me to fish this prestigious beat in lower water conditions less suitable for salmon.

The beat is known as Old Woman's which is also the name of the best salmon pool. Josh told me it was called this because an old woman used to come there to wash, but the story varies. Other versions have her drowning in the pool, which some of the locals call Dummon's Pit, Dummon being an old Devonshire word for an old woman or wife. The truth of the story, who she was and when and where she lived are long forgotten.

Just above the famous pool, Old Woman's Run lies between a high grassy bank on the right and a line of venerable old trees who lean inquisitively over the river from the left. The current was steady and it was not difficult to wade out to the thigh-deep centre from where I cast a nymph under boughs of oak and ash on the far side. It was a small green nymph with a gold head and a little sparkle. It swung round in the current and, with several upstream mends in the line, eventually finished its sweep downstream, from where I gathered the line to cast again. As the third cast swung round I felt a little nibble and lifted the rod smartly. Too fast for a downstream take and I missed the fish, probably pulled the fly out of his mouth, and reminded myself this kind of fishing is different to the upstream dry-fly tactics I practise more often.

After checking the fly I repeated the cast a couple more times and then felt another tug on the line. This time I was more restrained, lifted more steadily, and this time it worked. A silver fish motored around the river making the line thrum against the current and eventually submitted to my net. A fine rainbow trout which was probably an escapee from the fish farm a short distance upstream.

Rainbows are not supposed to be in the river, having been introduced to this country from America at the end of the nineteenth century, their ability to tolerate warmer water than brown trout makes them useful for stocking ponds and lakes. They are reared to be infertile so that escapees cannot establish free-living populations in the wild (though apparently this did happen on the Derbyshire Wye) but there is concern that these larger, non-native fish out-compete our wild brown trout for food and territory and eat eggs and fry of native fish. This is no doubt true, though they also do some good by eating invasive crayfish. I know this to be a fact because I have regularly found shattered remains of signal crayfish shells inside rainbow trout and the value of this service to the river is not to be underestimated.

Anyway, for the health of the river, policy is to remove them and I was pleased to do so. At the river's edge I tapped my fish on the head, wrapped him in dock leaves and hid him amongst tall grasses at the foot of the bank. If the day brought no further success, at least I had supper.

As I worked my way downstream, casting every few steps, I felt little nibbles from fish here and there so was encouraged to persevere with the same nymph and caught a couple of little brownies; small but sparkling with life, these wild fish were carefully returned to the river. Then, a short way further down I hooked another rainbow. An incredibly athletic fish of good size zipped around the river, passed me at a speed that made it plain he was not ready for the net, leaped clear of the water three times and then came off. Naturally, I was disappointed but my dismay was tempered by knowledge of a good fish already secured, so did not unduly despair. I praised the little nymph, who was blameless in the loss, tidied it up a bit and continued downstream. A wren like a fat bumblebee darted straight across the river to scuttle into the bank and large dragonflies quartered the river on wide glass-clear wings, hawking for prey, stalking insects as I was stalking trout.

Fishing here was a great privilege and whilst I love the wild waters of woods and moors it was refreshing to visit such a well managed, open beat where bankside bushes were pruned and ladders set in the bank to facilitate access at strategic points. This stretch of river was once owned by the Carnarvon Arms Hotel, which commanded five miles of fishing on the Exe and Barle and was conveniently situated about a mile from the junction of those two rivers, The Meeting of the Waters.

Arthur Applin who was a novelist, playwright and actor, recorded in his 1948 book, *Philandering Angler*, memories of staying at the Carnarvon Arms where he fished (and philandered) in far-off days of obscure innocence before the First World War. He remembered how an atmosphere of friendliness and freedom 'permeated every stone and stick in the place, together with the vagrant perfume of horses and stables; of wood smouldering in the grate; of bracken fern and freshly caught trout; and, when you turned the sheets on your bed, the sleep-compelling smell of lavender.'

When asking the hotel proprietor, Mr Nelder, about the size

of trout in the Exe, he was told, 'Mayn't take one under eight inches; a quarter pound's the average; half a pound is a good fish.'

Applin records how the clear, rippling streams held plenty of wild brown trout, Loch Levens from the Exe Valley trout farm and a few rainbows, so their presence in the river is nothing new. On his first visit he caught an outstandingly fine brown trout of just over two pounds and on one Easter Monday, during a prolific rise of blue uprights, caught an impressive thirteen trout in an hour.

Negley Farson, an American globetrotting fisherman, also wrote of fishing here in his 1942 *Going Fishing*, where, amongst tales of fishing all over the world, he describes this spot with special affection. 'It has a gentleness, a rich rustic worth, and an unostentatiousness that is like the English character. An imperturbable scene which fills you with contentment.'

He too, stayed at the famous Carnarvon Arms Hotel, where Old Woman's was one of the most popular beats. Farson recorded that you would be very lucky indeed if the trout you caught here averaged three to the pound and a half-pounder was a worthy accomplishment. Yet, although fish were never especially large, sport was outstanding. Fishermen from far and wide made pilgrimage to the hotel, where trays laden with fish would be arrayed on the hall table for admiration.

Old Woman's Beat is set amongst broad meadows sheltered on all sides by mounded hills; Hulverton Hill, Pixton Hill and Blight's Hill swell above the trees in rounded forms, their pastures dotted with sheep. On a sweeping right hand bend the river wraps around grass fields and is backed by tall oak, ash and sycamore on the far bank where a couple of back eddies are splattered white with slowly rotating foam. A natural shelf of rock cuts diagonally across the river and below this the bed drops away precipitously into the unfathomably deep Old Woman's Pool where the current turns over in a rolling wheel, churning back under itself. This had to be a good place for fish.

Certainly, Josh had assured me, it was a good place for salmon. Running up river during a spate they might pause here to gather strength before facing fast water hammering over riffles above and sometimes, if the spate suddenly drops off, they become trapped and must wait for water to rise again. If salmon liked this cool, well oxygenated pool, I reasoned, so might trout.

So I cast across the bend and let the current carry my nymph downstream, over the lip of rock into deep water below. As it passed the first back eddy there was a huge swirl and splash as if something large had seen it, recognised the subterfuge and was expressing scorn. Even anger. The line swirled in the churning green depths and was impossible to keep straight until it was drawn downstream when, having almost reached its furthest hang, it went dead. It was caught on a rock, I thought, pulling at it ineffectually.

Then it moved.

I lifted my rod and felt life on the end of the line which zig zagged around, cutting into water too deeply to see what was attached. Whatever it was bent the rod over, energetically angulating about the pool. When the fish eventually came close enough to the surface to be visible I pulled the net off my shoulders but was unable to get into a position to reach him in the deep water. Could I pull him up over the rocky shelf-edge towards me or would he come off in the fast water of the fall, I wondered. There was no alternative but to try.

Miraculously, he stayed on and in the shallower, smoother water I could see I had hooked a magnificent rainbow as he zipped past me heading upstream. This bid for freedom was soon checked and as he came back to me I was ready with the net but he was not to be easily caught. Three times he passed me whilst skilfully avoiding my net; he was too long for it, he thrashed violently and I wished I had brought a larger one. (Such sweet regret.) On the fourth pass I managed to scoop him in head first, spotted tail flopping over the rim, and as I carried him to the bank he spat out the hook. Gleaming silver and pink speckled with black, he was a spectacular fish and I thanked the river for such a bountiful gift. What a feast he would make.

Rainbows from the river have a far superior flavour and texture to those from still waters and I am always delighted to catch one to take home for the table, their status as intruders in a habitat where they do not belong absolving me from any doubt as to the morality of killing them. And they offer some cracking sport.

The splendid fishing at Old Woman's is further enhanced by the convenience of an inn alongside the river at the top of the beat. Sadly, the welcoming doors of the Carnarvon Arms have long been closed but here, at the Anchor Inn, you can still sit at a bench on the riverbank, as Applin and Farson both did, to enjoy a refreshing glass of ale at the end of a day's fishing. Well, what would you have done?

CHAPTER 28

A Morning for the River

———

Three men stood on the riverside track, shoulders hunched and collars turned against the weather, calling cheery greetings from below dripping hat brims. As I slithered to a halt beside them, heavy August rain hammered into the mud and showed no sign of abating while I struggled into thigh waders and dragged on two raincoats, sticky and clingy with wet as soon as I stepped out of my vehicle. We had gathered in response to a call from Dulverton Angling Association to help carry out some river management work on the Little Exe, an inexpert but willing team, our numbers soon swelled to five; all of us regularly fished nearby beats and cared enough about the river to turn up on a wet Saturday morning. Alistair issued ropes, saws, loppers and various other tools which we carried along the riverbank and as we walked he explained the object of our work.

Puzzlecombe Copse is mixed woodland standing on a steep hillside sloping down to the western bank of the River Exe. Along its lower margin a strip of newly cleared land some twenty five paces wide between the riverbank and the trees was a mangled mess of brash and branches half buried in mud by the tracks of heavy forestry machinery.

"The Angling Association engaged forestry contractors to cut out a strip of trees along the bottom of the plantation here,"

Alistair told us. "Useful timber has been removed by the estate and we're going to tidy up the rest."

As we splodged through the mud he explained that a band of tall, tightly spaced conifers had grown close to the riverbank casting a uniform shade for the length of the plantation. Shade had stretched across the whole width of the watercourse making the river cold and dark which suppressed the growth of vegetation, leaving bare soil vulnerable to erosion and a rather sterile riverbank environment.

"Nothing could grow under those conifers," Alistair said, putting down a heavy box of gear. "What we are aiming to do is to allow sunlight to reach the river and encourage this bare ground to develop growth."

So we began the process of clearing up – dragging branches out of the mud, cutting up sticks, heaping into manageable piles and making fires. Some piles were left to rot away naturally. They would quickly be colonised by the fungi and bacteria that live on rotting wood while insects and hedgehogs could take shelter inside them.

"Will this area be replanted?" I asked, looking around at the desolate stretch of mud and brash.

"No. It will be allowed to regenerate naturally. It will quickly grow over because there will be more sunlight now. The bank and the river need light."

I imagined how it might develop: at first there would be a flush of flowering herbs and grasses, then brambles and patches of scrub and eventually some trees. Hopefully, most of these would be native species which would support local invertebrates. With the blessing of sunlight, herbs and low scrub along the riverbank could thrive, their roots binding soil in the bank and their flowers providing pollen and nectar to attract insects.

It wasn't long before raincoats were shed as we warmed to our task and decided it was less uncomfortable just to be wet than to be wet and hot. The hope of keeping dry had long been abandoned. We seemed to work pretty well together as a team

– everyone was sensible and careful and if I brought no chainsaw and little muscle to the job, I was able to drag smaller branches, coil ropes, fetch things and hoped I was of some use.

When we had three bonfires burning merrily we set to work at a place where a diseased ash tree growing from the edge of the bank had fallen into the river. It was partially hung up in branches of other trees and its falling had bent saplings into a pressurised bow waiting to spring. We fixed ropes on the fallen tree and four of us hauled on it. It didn't move. I suggested bringing a vehicle up the track to supply a bit more power, although I really thought a draught horse might have been more useful and could have also worked in the river. It was decided, no doubt correctly, that a vehicle would get stuck in the mud and although a horse might be helpful we did not have one. We would have to rely upon our own strength.

Alistair took a chainsaw to the problem. Impressively turned out in protective chainsaw gear over chest waders, he cut off one or two major branches and a couple of saplings enabling the whole tangle to be dismantled. Then we pulled the timber in with ropes, using the power of the current to swing long poles around to where they could be secured alongside the bank. The biggest poles, such as the main ash trunk, were tied in with steel hawser and lashed to live alder stumps. Smaller pieces were pushed in behind them, pinned into place with interlocking branches, forked behind stumps, entwined together in a huge bundle like a massive faggot. It would not easily be moved even in high water.

Left where it had fallen, the next spate would have carried the tree away. If that happened it could damage the downstream bridge, or might lodge underneath it, trap debris and create a dam which would cause flooding. Securing the tree safely meant it could be kept in the river without causing problems. Fallen wood in the edge of the river provides food and shelter for aquatic invertebrates and fish fry, and the way it was positioned would deflect the current and reinforce the bank.

Amongst the boxes of gear we found flasks of hot water and jars of coffee – just what we wanted. As I filled mugs and passed them around, we discussed how the ash tree lying alongside the bank would affect the physical processes of the river. The sticks against the bank would trap silt where new vegetation could take root, effectively advancing the riverbank forwards and pinching the channel a little narrower.

"So there will be a stretch of faster water?" I asked.

"Exactly." Alistair swallowed hot coffee with a look of satisfaction. "It will be better oxygenated and will scour the gravel clean."

After our coffee break chainsaws revved up again and two-stroke exhaust fumes mingled with woodsmoke hanging in the moist air. A length of about fifteen or twenty paces of riverbank was cleared of overhanging bushes to allow light to fall on a clattering riffle. Sunlight will encourage underwater weed and algae which will oxygenate the water and provide food and cover for lots of wildlife. Many invertebrates such as nymphs of mayfly, stonefly and caddis as well as snails, tadpoles and many other aquatic creatures graze on weed and algae. Trout spawn in riffles, and when fry emerge they need easy access to such invertebrates for food and weedy cover to hide from predators without travelling far. Sunlight kindles life.

The trees we cut down were not killed but coppiced. Stumps of around a foot high were left with smooth, sloping cuts to shed water cleanly, avoiding rot. Each stump will sprout again with many new shoots arising from the base to form a dense bush. Some thinner stems of alder and hazel were cut part way through, leaving a hinge on which they were bent back over and laid downstream, into the side of the bank, like laying a hedge. In both cases the roots will survive to continue their valuable role of binding together the soil of the riverbank.

It is vital to retain some bankside trees, of course – in summer, when flow is low, a river with no shade quickly becomes overheated and deoxygenated. The most important place for shade is over deep pools where the slow water has no turbulence to incorporate oxygen, and these cool, dark depths are favoured haunts held by the biggest fish. Trees deliver a rich supply of nutrients to the river. Fish love to feed on all manner of mis-adventurous beetles, spiders and caterpillars as they fall from overhanging branches; then each autumn the water is strewn with fallen leaves which, in decomposing, provide food for aquatic creatures such as freshwater shrimps and caddis larvae, which in turn are food for dippers and trout. Trout need both trees and sunlight.

"Ideally, we should aim to have around eighty percent sun-light on riffles and eighty percent shade on deep pools", Alistair said. The work we had carried out had moved this stretch of river towards that optimum balance.

Rivers naturally include a wide range of conditions; straight runs where fast water maintains a clean, stony bed and bends with slow, deep pools and muddy bottoms; steeply washed out banks on the outside of bends and shallow beaches where gravel accumulates on the inside. Every different situation creates a habitat unlike the others and each area is needed by different wildlife species, or by a species at different stages of its life. Every variation of conditions is valuable.

In the past, rivers have been pushed aside and tidied away for human convenience – their meanders straightened, multiple streams restricted into a single channel, wriggling convolutions sprawling across fields have been contained and straightjack-eted. Rivers are wild and wilful and often cause problems for those trying to wrest uncertain livings from changeable riverside land. The natural sway of a river is inconvenient to landown-ers for whom river channels often form boundaries which are not intended to move. Left to run on their own ways, rivers can steal land from productive fields, dangerously undermine roads and make areas unmanageable by placing them beyond reach within tight bends or on islands between divided streams. This unruly behaviour is seldom allowed to continue unchecked but straight, regulated rivers have few variations in depth or flow so restricting the area occupied by rivers has limited not just their extent but, especially, the range of habitats within them and the wildlife they can support.

Our morning's work was designed to oppose the trend of homogenisation by creating more variation in depth and flow and in light and shade, all of which would increase the availability of food and cover for small aquatic lives. It felt good to redress a little of the balance in favour of the river. We went home for lunch tired and wet but satisfied that we had spent our morning doing a useful job and given a little back to the river that gives us all so much.

CHAPTER 29

A Famous Fly

Tiverton is a Devon market town, though there is no longer a livestock market, and if the centre appears dominated by rather plain shops there are also a few interesting ones and the elegant church and vigorous façade of the town hall remember more prosperous times. It is a decidedly rural town and when the wind is in the west, which it so often is, the refrain of the Tiverton Fox Hounds singing in their kennels, drifts between the chimney pots.

In the late nineteenth century there lived in the town a Mr Robert Stanway Austin. He kept a shop at 19 Gold Street, advertising himself as a tobacconist and fishing tackle maker, from where, on warm summer evenings he would slip down to the river to fish. It was only a short walk from the back door of his shop, away from the clamorous bustle of the town to the peace of the riverside meadows.

Here on the River Exe he tried out flies he had designed and created. In those not so very far-off days there were few synthetic materials – there was no antron, no mylar, nylon and polyester had yet to be invented. Fly tying depended upon the use of natural, locally available ingredients. This was, no doubt, limiting in many respects but it gave fishing flies a provenance and character as distinctive as the burred speech of the craftsmen and women who made them.

Mr Austin was an accomplished angler and fly tier yet he might have remained in obscurity, unheard of outside Tiverton and unremembered much beyond his death, had it not been for his friendship, developed through a series of written correspondence, with the fishing writer G.E.M. Skues.

One evening in early summer Robert Austin picked up his rod, put a tin of flies in his pocket and walked through the backstreets of Tiverton, past Ford's Brewery and St Andrew's Mill, to the Lowman Pool where the little River Lowman enters the River Exe, just above the field known as The Rag. He tried a new fly of his own design and making, simply to see whether it was any good. To his surprise he caught six fish weighing a total of four and three quarter pounds with the biggest at one pound seven ounces. He must have wondered whether it was a fluke, perhaps the trout were feeding particularly voraciously that day, as he knew they sometimes can, so he went back the next evening to be sure. On the second occasion he had four fish weighing five pounds in all, including one of three pounds and half an ounce. These were great fish for the Exe, their presence must have been noted by other fishermen of the town and they would certainly not have remained in the pool had they been catchable. But fish only live to reach such sizes through cunning and no one had yet offered them a fly they would take. Mr Austin's fly was something special.

It was around June 1900 when Mr Austin wrote to George Skues telling him of this success and enclosing his original fly on its now broken Limerick eyed hook. Skues was intrigued and when returning the fly he asked about its prescription. Austin was sufficiently generous to tell him the ingredients and even sent a little of the dubbing mixture so that Skues could make some flies of his own, but was shrewd enough to swear him to secrecy. A successful and inimitable fly could be the making of his little business.

Mr Austin's original notes written in 1900 described the fly as being 'dressed with full yellow silk, buzz, on an 00 (16) Pennell hook, with a blue hackle of a lighter colour and freckled thickly with gold. Body of a mixture of ram's wool, cream coloured seal's fur, lemon spaniel fur, and a few pinches of yellow mohair.' Skues suggested using crimson seal's fur instead of mohair and Austin accepted and adopted the idea. He noted a small yellow tip, very conspicuous in natural flies, and regarded it as a desirable feature in the imitation. Skues recommended a tail of honey dun or bright, light blue spade feather although Austin had written, 'I do not call the yellow at the end of the Tup a tag. It is hardly big enough for that.'

Austin had not named the fly and it was Skues who called it the Tup's Indispensable and wrote of its virtues in his column for the *Fishing Gazette* as well as, later, in his various books about fly fishing including *Minor Tactics of the Chalk Stream* and *Itchen Memories*, describing its appearance without giving away the secret ingredients.

Skues made copies of this innovative fly and fished it on his home river, the Itchen, where fished wet or dry it proved as successful as it had on the Exe. He wrote:

For wet fly purposes this is as much of the dressing as I am at liberty to give: Primrose tying silk lapped down the hook from head to tail, a pale blue or creamy whisk of hen's feather as soft as possible and not long, three or four turns of coarser untwisted primrose sewing silk at the tail, body rather fat, of a mixed dubbing of a creamy pink and a soft blue dun hackle, very short in the fibre, at the head, the dressing being preferably finished at the shoulder behind the hackle. When this fly is thoroughly soaked it has a wonderfully soft and translucent, insect like effect.

There was only one place to obtain a genuine example of this marvellous fly. The Tiverton shop took orders for hundreds of dozens and poor Mr Austin became quite exhausted by tying them. His daughter, Agnes, helped in this task and went on making the flies and keeping the secret of their ingredients long after her father had died. It was only when she herself retired that she finally gave permission for the formula to be published. Skues clearly had great respect for Mr Austin, crediting him with 'first hand knowledge of the river and its flies' and noting, 'his conscience will not let him put up with, and issue to his customers inadequate materials.' It was doubtless Skues' promotion that brought the fly to the attention of anglers the world over. It was the brilliance of Austin's design that held it there.

The fame of the Tup's Indispensable grew as the fly spread all over the world, proving equally deadly on rivers across Europe, Africa and America. It is still frequently used by anglers today, though is generally made from artificial materials and often in lurid colours. Few people attempt the original ingredients, preferring to use more easily obtained, manufactured materials. I, however, was not so easily satisfied.

The main difficulty in obtaining Austin's original ingredients is that the ram's wool, for which the fly is named, must be taken from the animal's testicles. Wool there is finer, lighter than that over the rest of the ram's body and has a delicate primrose tinge which is doubtless a staining of urine. The smell is distinctly ovine. Imagine trying to buy such a substance on the internet.

A young friend, Oliver, runs a team of contract shearers who travel all over Exmoor visiting different flocks. He was clearly in a position to obtain the necessary material and, to my delight, was not only unperturbed by my request but willing to provide it. In only a few days I received a message to let me know he had the required stuff.

It was a dark winter evening when I met Oliver in a pub halfway between our two homes. As we sipped cider beside the fire he handed over a package wrapped in plain brown paper. We must have looked suspicious. If anyone had enquired, I doubt our explanations would have dispelled their concerns.

Mr Austin wrote, 'I always wash the wool from a tup as it is almost invariably unfit unless you do. The floating power of the fly is not injured by this process if it be dressed with a good hackle and touched slightly with paraffin . . . indeed, I fancy it would take a vast amount of washing to get all the natural grease out of the wool.' I used a small net that had once contained oranges to hold the wool while I squeezed it out in warm water with a little plain soap, washing it only enough to remove the dung and hoping to retain the natural lanolin grease. It was then patted with kitchen paper and spread out on newspaper to dry in the sun.

The procurement of lemon spaniel's fur was a far simpler matter. I walked up over the fields to visit my neighbour, Victoria, who has the most scampery, waggly lemon and white spaniel called Gladys. In asking for a little hair I rather expected it to be combed from a brush next time the dog was groomed but Victoria was more pragmatic. She pinned down the wriggling, protesting Gladys and plucked away at her curly ears until I insisted that was enough. So I walked home with a pocketful of lemon spaniel fur.

John Dawson, a fishing guide from Bampton, has run a fly tying club for some twenty years. The group meets fortnightly to develop their skills, dress some flies and exchange stories (some of them, no doubt, true) about fishing. When unable to meet in real life, due to Covid restrictions, we met in the virtual world and tied flies at home. On one such occasion when John could not be with us I suggested that we tie a Tup's Indispensable and the idea was met with general agreement, especially as one member, Dee, had recently enjoyed considerable success with a beaded version on both a lake and on the River Barle. So as I set out to make my Tup's I was encouraged by the support of others dressing the same fly at the same time.

That evening a wild wind came hurtling through the trees to rampage around the house. It blasted down the chimney, puffed ash out of the fireplace and filled the room with smoke as I gathered together my materials and laid out my tools. Tying fishing flies is a mysterious and satisfying alchemy; much hope and expectation may be found in weaving together a carefully chosen selection of ingredients to create tiny charms with the magical potential to summon fish. It is intricate, detailed work.

My little fly tying desk in a corner is a quiet, focussed place to work and sitting before it I turn my back on the rest of the room. I took a pinch of tup's wool and a wisp of golden spaniel fur, sandwiching them together and teasing the fibres apart, over and over, until they amalgamated into a homogenous, pale yellowish fluff for a dubbing. Then a second mixture was made in the same way using creamy tup's wool with a few fibres of burgundy hare's ear and scarlet rabbit fur, in place of the mohair I didn't have, to create a pink dubbing. These materials would form the body of the fly.

The subtle craft of creating such an artifice calls for dexterity, patience and, yes, a certain cunning. A fishing fly is, after all, a trick, and for it to be effective its appearance must be considered from a trout's perspective. If it is to work it must be mistaken for a real insect by a wild creature whose daily life depends upon identifying insects and it must function in an underwater environment so alien to us that we could not survive there for more than a few minutes. It is a deceit, but one whose practice brings us a deeper understanding of the fish to whom it will be offered.

John Dawson had given me some old dry-fly hooks; small, fine, bronze coloured hooks with elegant curves. He told me they had been made pre 1930 and were equivalent to today's size fourteen or sixteen. With the tiny hook held in a vice, maintaining a soft, regular tension with the bobbin, a thread of primrose silk was spiralled along the shaft. Just before the bend I tied in a fine wisp of golden feather to make a tail, only the tips of three or four barbs; the merest suggestion of a tail.

Then, holding the silk taut, I rubbed it with beeswax, sliding the sharp lip of a candle stub up and down the thread. You must rub quickly, creating a little friction which warms the wax just sufficiently for it to soften and meld onto the silk. With the thread waxed, a tiny pinch of yellow dubbing can be spun onto it between finger and thumb, to be wound around the shaft of the hook two or three times. Next a pinch of the pink dubbing is bound around the shaft, and I let it grow a little thicker as I worked forwards towards the eye of the hook. This would form the thorax of the fly.

Fly dressing must be practised with a calm, focussed intention that usefully spills over into other aspects of life. It is an art of essentially slow ritual that cannot be hurried; the components have to be bound together with infinite care and concentration, imparting strength as well as delicacy to the minute construction.

The thread hung down from the hook, held in place by the weight of its bobbin, as I searched for a suitable feather to make the hackle. A hackle is a whorl of radiating fibres which will hold a dry fly up on the surface of the water or undulate around a wet fly's thorax and which it is hoped, in a trout's eye view, might appear similar to insect legs. I chose a feather, selected for size by bending it to make the barbs stand out and offering them up against the little hook until I found a feather with barbs of a length to match it. Fluffy barbs at the base of the feather were pulled away to leave a clean quill. Once attached, I snipped off the stub and wound the feather around the shaft, just behind the eye. As the quill turned around the hook the barbs stood out like spokes encircling the shaft and after three turns I tied in the end of the feather and whipped the thread around the top of the shaft a few times to form a yellow head. The whole fly, including its tail, measured less than half an inch.

Each member of the group used whatever materials and hooks they had to hand so, although we all worked to a common pattern it was interpreted imaginatively and everyone produced something a little different. Fred used sheep's wool with red and yellow seal fur, Ian made two dry and two wet versions, Dave's had red in the hackle, Peter made a sparkly one, then another as a beaded nymph, Neil made a Tup's Diawl Bach with a throat hackle and Dee added metallic bead heads. Given the available materials, I tried to make mine as close to the original as possible though regretted I had never seen the genuine article. When we had dressed our flies, photos of them were exchanged on WhatsApp accompanied by the inevitable banter about the delicate parts of a ram.

Fred added, 'I bet Mr Austin in his Tiverton tobacconist shop didn't imagine we would all be here tying his fly 120 years later.'

No, I bet he didn't.

The Tiverton Fly Fishing Association has beats covering some four miles of the River Exe between Cove and Bickleigh including a stretch of river passing through the town. It is through membership of this organisation I have access to fish the Lowman Pool, though I had never done so before, usually preferring more rural stretches away from the town. But on this occasion I wanted to return the Tiverton fly to its place of birth, to cast a Tup's Indispensable upon its home waters out of curiosity, perhaps with a sense of ceremony and tradition and to see whether it could still work its special magic.

A long meadow called the Rag Field stretches to the lower end of the beat, and there I began to fish and to work my way slowly upstream. The town was not far off but noise of traffic was washed away by the sound of the river. About a third of the way up I waded into a shallow ford where tractors had been crossing between meadows on either side. The banks were obscured by balsam, nettles and brambles heavy with blackberries, the pebbly bottom was a little brown and gungey though offered a good footing, but a gusty breeze blowing across the river hampered my casting. Water on the other side was deeper, weedier with the bubble line close under the far bank so I worked hard to get my little Tup's fly across. Wind tossed it playfully back.

Just upstream of the ford an old ash leaned over the river, listening to the murmuring current, trailing finger-like twigs in the water; and below the trailing twigs a bright body leapt clear of the surface, glinting silver against dark green foliage. I put the fly over that spot and the fish rose to it but didn't take. So I left him for a while and cast up the centre of the river a few times, pulling in line fast to maintain contact with the fly as it was swept towards me on the hastening current. A grey wagtail swooped past, whistling gleefully but no fish showed any sign of interest.

Then I put my fly beside the ash twigs again. It drifted down two, maybe three feet before silver wheeled below the surface, I lifted the rod and felt a nice weight on the line. As he circled the pool I managed to keep the line taut while dragging the net off my shoulder, stretching the elastic lanyard and twanging it off over my hat. As I drew him steadily closer I saw that the fish was a smart grayling with regimented rows of mirror-bright, metallic scales and a long crimson dorsal fin. I held out my net to receive him with gratitude.

After paying my respects to the handsome grayling and watching him swirl back into the current, I sat on the bank to eat some dark chocolate and a handful of blackberries (a delicious combination, you really must try) and listened to the voice of the river. Bees and hoverflies hummed around the powdery-scented Himalayan balsam and a few duck flew languidly upstream.

In a little while I moved on and tried one or two other spots before reaching the end of the meadow but did not contact any more fish there. From the field gate I followed a path along the riverbank and in a short distance came to the Lowman Pool. The River Lowman rises near the radar tower, locally known as The Golfball, at Cobbacombe Cross, up in the hills of Bampton Down. It winds through Huntsham, Uplowman, and the delightfully named Craze Lowman where it becomes especially wiggly. On its approach to the grand River Exe the Lowman is quiet and deferential as it moves through thickly treed banks, darkened with holly, hung with ivy, giving a woodland feel to the shady stream's course. The head of the Lowman Pool is formed by a bar of rock slanting across the river to create a natural weir. Above it the water was like glass, gliding serenely between tall ash, sycamore and lime, as calm as an empty church. When water reached the weir it accelerated into a slide, plunging into the white maelstrom churning below.

I crept along a rocky ledge at the side of the pool, restrained by the sheer drop into bottomless fast water at its edge. Sycamore and buddleia reached overhead, limiting the upward reach of my rod, so I tried a few roll casts, sending my little Tup's Indispensable towards the foot of the weir. Turbulence snatched the line away instantly. In that crashing water I thought it likely any fish would be too deep to reach and even using a weighted fly would have made little difference.

Then I felt something tugging at the line the way a child might tug at your jacket hem, calling to you, small but insistent, demanding your attention. I lifted the rod and it bent in half. The grey, kype-jawed neb of a salmon broke the surface and I knew I was both outclassed and outgunned. This was a big fish. Huge. I would have to be very delicate with my three pound leader and three weight rod.

The fish moved downstream through the deepest, strongest part of the river and I tried to allow him a little line without losing tension. For one instant I saw my rod bending like a rainbow over the Lowman Pool, arcing above white foam tumbling over dark khaki water, bowing under boughs of canopies aglow with the first light gilding of autumn. My awareness panned out to a wide span, wider than a century, to imagine Mr Austin fishing here so many years ago feeling a similar thrill and to wonder at how his incredible, world-famous fly had stood the test of years and was, even today, connecting me to this supremely awesome fish in the vortex of this very pool where its long life began and to see myself, a small figure in a brown hat, under the stately trees beside the roaring waters of this mighty eternal river. All this vision concentrated into seconds. For one brief, glorious moment there was splendour – and then he was gone. I reeled the line in unharmed, the leader intact, the fish had simply spat out my little fly leaving me bereft yet still elated with, however briefly tasted, the unforgettable feeling of his wild power.

Just then, a kingfisher arrowed up the river in a streak of sapphire laughter.

Footnote:

The recipe for the Tup's Indispensable was first published in the *Flyfishers' Journal* 1934, in an article written by G.E.M. Skues. He reported Austin's early success with the fly as securing, '. . . in two or three successive evenings a number of big trout which the natives there counted uncatchable, one of them exceeding 5lb.; another 3lb. ½oz. ; another 2 ½lb.; and another about 2lb.'

However, Alfred Courtney Williams, in his 1973 *Dictionary of Trout Flies*, writes that he had access to Austin's original notes and letters from which he quotes, 'The first evening I used this fly I got six fish, weighing 4¾ lb. in the pool at the top of the Kag; biggest fish 1lb. 7oz. The next night I had four weighing 5lb., biggest fish 3lb. ½oz.'

Although things may have been different in those far-off days, I have to say, I think an Exe trout exceeding five pounds most unlikely and, much as I hesitate to doubt the founding father of nymph fishing, I am inclined to believe Williams. Although Skues had the more direct contact it was thirty four years later he wrote of it.

Courtney Williams was wrong about the name of the field and adjacent stretch of river just below Tiverton, which is not called the Kag but the Rag. This is almost certainly a misinterpretation of Austin's handwriting; it is understandable that he might have mistaken a capital letter R for a K in an unfamiliar script. Nevertheless, he must have seen the original handwritten letter to have done so.

CHAPTER 30

Redford Bottom

Through gorse bristling taller than myself, I clambered down across a rough track to approach a ford, with low winter sun in my eyes glinting from the water's faceted surface. Redford Bottom is a long combe, chiselled sharply into moorland between heather and moor grass, the south facing cleave thickly clad with deer-sheltering gorse and the boggy valley bottom sedgy, peaty and deep. One of the few places to get safely across this combe between Brimblecombe Hill and Moorhouse Ridge is known as Redford Crossing.

On either side of the wide shallow ford the stream whittles its way between tussocks of rushes and sedges, undercutting the peaty sward to leave unstable banks, overhanging like eaves, thatched with roots. Chunks of bank, broken away from the land on either side, are left stranded as small islands in the divided flow and I jumped between them to cross the fast, deep current. As I did so my shadow flicked across the water and two dark cigar shapes darted away from the centre of the ford. I scolded myself for such thoughtlessness. It had been impossible to see into the water while facing the sun and difficult to reach the other side but there were fish here and they had seen me before I saw them – the cardinal sin. As a penalty the fish were gone, arrowing away upstream into fast water where the ground was too deep to follow.

I had read how spawning trout travel upstream in search of cool, well oxygenated water in fast flowing streams with a substrate of clean gravel pieces small enough for them to move. Little rapid streams like this are cool in winter and spring, though they can be at risk of overheating and drought in summer, but their restricted size limits the ability of large predators to live there, so a small stream is a safer nursery for young fry. Such a soft, tasty morsel as a tiny trout is always vulnerable in a hungry world so they need plenty of cover like weed streaming in the current or overhanging from the banks, just downstream and within easy reach of where they are hatched. This place should be ideal.

After watching more discreetly for a few minutes I decided those fish were not coming back; at least, not yet. So I ventured closer and waded into the edge of the ford from where I could see the pebbly bottom below shallow tea coloured water. The redd was very clear; a pit freshly scooped into the golden brown stream bed with excavated pebbles piled into a heap on the downstream side. The hollow nest was about eight or nine inches long, a similar length to the two trout I had seen leaving it. And scanning the width of the ford I could see there were others, less fresh and distinct but, viewed beside this obvious one as a measure, almost certainly the same.

I climbed out of the combe and wandered over Moorhouse Ridge towards Soggy Moor along the clear, weed-waved depths of a leat that takes water to Lyshwell Farm and here and there, where I could reach it, peered between tussocks into the darkly gurgling stream.

Further up Redford Bottom there is another crossing where land swells into low mounds to the south west and clusters of thorn trees offer scant cover for deer and black cattle who loaf around between them. There is no substantial track here but paths from all directions converge on the ford; narrow hoof-carved ways cut into the red soil leaving gravel in the washed-out bottoms. On the wide ford the water boiled and as my eyes focussed I saw half a dozen or so largish trout scurrying away through water too shallow to cover their backs. They did not stay in view long but it was good to find them, to know how the stream seethes with the focussed energy of a passion to perpetuate life.

Trout spawning rate is determined by size and age of fish, and is also influenced by nutrition and physical stress. Brown trout typically produce 700 to 900 eggs per pound of body weight; older fish often producing fewer but larger eggs which may have a higher chance of survival. Clearly, there is usually a high failure rate but must be potential for rapid population expansion in streams offering suitable conditions for young trout to thrive. Numbers of fish might be suppressed by limited food or excess predation, but if the general health of a stream could be improved there is hope for prodigious resurgence.

Towards the headwaters, the valley becomes wider, shallower and then ceases to be a valley at all; the arterial stream divided into fine, capillary-like trickles oozing through the land. As stream became bog I decided conditions were becoming increasingly unsuitable for spawning fish so turned away to walk back over the hill. Snipe rose with brief, clipped squawks, flittering away towards Cloggs Farm on pale tapered wings, and a thorn tree streaming with lichens held aloft the cluster of sticks arranged there by a crow last spring. A group of Exmoor ponies smelling warm and sweet as a hayfield watched me pass between them, the uncertain youngsters erect-necked and high stepping, their mothers uninterested and relaxed.

When I got back to Redford Crossing I was extremely careful, as I should have been the first time, to keep my shadow off the water and to maintain a low, stooping profile. A little further up the stream, with a bit of a scramble, I found a way of crossing to the south side, circled around cautiously in the stuggy ground and approached the ford with a suitably respectable bow. I sat on a tussock of rushes, ate some chocolate and watched the water.

I wondered where these fish had come from to spawn here;

did they spend their lives in the deeper pools of this stream or had they come up from the Danesbrook, or the Barle? How far had they journeyed, forcing their way against the swift current to reach this place so perfectly suited to enable their eggs to develop and their young to grow. And what of the young trout who might hatch here? How far away might they travel? Several hundred, maybe thousands, might hatch in these redds but the little stream will hold insufficient nutrition for them all so they must disperse widely in search of food. A few may stay nearby, others might venture a long way downstream, some to the Danesbrook, the Barle or maybe as far as the Exe and some, perhaps, even reaching the sea. A fish tracking study on the River Deveron in Scotland found that trout, who never went to sea, travelled astonishing distances up and down the river. One twenty two inch hen fish migrated fifty two miles downstream, apparently in search of richer feeding, before returning to spawn. Wherever they go from here, those few trout who survive to become adults may one day remember their moorland home and make their way back towards this little stream in Redford Bottom to spawn children of their own.

The rushes were cold and damp and by the time my chocolate was finished I had to move my seizing joints and walk smartly up the hill to get warm. I hadn't seen any more fish.

I had always thought Redford Crossing a tautology – a ford being a crossing, Red Ford is all that is necessary but, though marked as such on the map, I had never heard anyone call it that. And then I thought, maybe this place was not named, as I had always assumed, after the colour of the earth which, through a collaboration of hooves and water, has eroded to expose the rather reddish soil lying below the dark peaty land around it. But perhaps this was originally Redd Ford. Wouldn't it be nice to think so.

CHAPTER 31

Freeing the Flow

A sheet of white water cascades over a slope like the pitched roofs of a row of houses slanting across the River Exe. On the far side of this colossal weir lie broad grass fields grazed by dairy cattle, a train sways along the main line approaching the city and beyond that Stoke Woods rise to a cloud-mottled sky. At the foot of the weir foam-flecked dark water swirls around a wide pool and from its invisible depths a majestic salmon leaps clear of the water, body arched tense with effort, broad tail flapping uselessly at air, only to fall back into churning foam. Pynes Weir, just above Exeter, is a formidable obstacle requiring supreme strength, stamina and determination in salmon and sea trout attempting to travel upstream to spawn. Many never make it.

In lowest water conditions fish cannot even reach this weir as they get stuck at the first obstacle in the river, Trews Weir, in the city of Exeter. Then, after a few showery days the flow increases a little allowing some progress and small fish can move, but on a sloping weir like this larger fish still cannot find enough water to cover their backs.

At the end of a droughty summer much of the weir face is still dry, grasses take root in broken concrete and water sliding over the shoulders of the massive structure is so shallow that dippers bob in and out to feed. In the weir pool below, salmon gather in serried ranks, all aligned with the swirling current, waiting. Some fish have tried to fling themselves forward onto the thin sheet of hissing water but have fallen back, sometimes injured, always exhausted, while other fish seem to know the feat is beyond their strength, so they all wait. They wait for rain.

Summer fades, hips and haws turn scarlet, pale bones of hogweed and dock stems like rusted iron stand on the bank but no rains come. In a dry autumn fish may have to wait here for weeks or months and in this crowded pool they are vulnerable to human and animal predation and to disease. Pollution from throughout the catchment accumulates in the lower reaches of the river and when the volume of water is reduced it becomes concentrated and can strip the water of oxygen. This is not a healthy place to linger.

When rains finally quench the parched earth and fill the river with a coffee coloured surge, fish can move upstream at last. First there is just enough water for small fish to pass over obstacles, then with rising river levels increasingly larger fish find the depth they need but, as the spate grows and velocity builds, smaller fish are unable to face the crashing power of the current. For each fish size there is an optimum water level for easiest ascent, but periods of ideal flow do not last long; the changing climate is bringing more extremes of drought and flood, restricting times of moderate flow and making fish passage ever more difficult. As periods of low water are lasting longer, weirs are favouring smaller fish which produce fewer eggs so we expect the next generations of salmon to be reduced in both number and size. However, in any water conditions Pynes Weir is thought to be impassable for fish of less than a couple of feet long as they simply lack the necessary strength.

Weirs present a tough challenge to migratory fish. Natural barriers such as rock formations are less insurmountable because water plunging over the top and pounding into the pool below, possibly over thousands of years, gradually erodes the riverbed to create a deep pool. Manmade structures have not been in place long enough for this to occur and many are artificially maintained to prevent it happening at all. Fish need a pool at least as deep as the height of the obstacle ahead to generate the acceleration and propulsion necessary to power over it. Also, natural barriers usually have a rough uneven surface which creates differences in the current including, within the tumult, pockets of sheltered quieter water allowing fish to get a sort of fin-hold to help them up, but a smooth weir face like this one has an unbroken, unremitting sheet of falling water which, offering no opportunity to pause, must be ascended in one herculean effort.

The ceaseless power of the River Exe has long been harnessed for human industry. Mills operating on the river were reported in the Domesday Book and continued to grind corn into flour and to manufacture paper and cloth until the running water they relied upon was replaced by motors and electricity. Mill owners forced the river into hard labour for their own profit and repaid the service ungraciously by polluting its waters with their effluent, depleting its life-force by abstraction and impeding its course with their weirs.

Weirs were built to maintain a head of water in a strategic position to service a leat, usually for the function of turning a mill wheel. The leat generally discharged into the river a little lower down, returning the borrowed water but leaving an intersecting stretch of riverbed parched, including the face of the weir itself. Today few mills continue to operate on water power but weirs remain, a few are managed to extract water for fish farms and various other purposes but most are redundant industrial waste; those who profited from their use simply walking (or more probably riding) away unconcerned, unrepentant.

One morning on the river I met Phil Turnbull who is Fisheries Technical Officer for the Westcountry Rivers Trust. As we walked along the riverbank he told me about the Strategic Exe Weirs project he manages, which seeks to tackle this problem.

Phil explained that there are eleven intact weirs causing major difficulties for migrating fish attempting to pass up or down the River Exe. Even small impacts of apparently passable weirs can quickly add up to a massive cumulative effect. Assuming a generous ninety percent success rate at each of eleven weirs means only thirty one percent of fish entering the Exe Estuary will reach Exmoor.

The Exe and Barle used to be famous salmon rivers; fishermen came from miles around to fish here but we have less than a fifth of the numbers we had seventy years ago and River Exe salmon are now officially designated as 'at risk'. Make no mistake, that means at risk of extinction.

Migratory salmon face a daunting barrage of threats beginning in the river of their birth. Smolts delayed by weirs in their down-stream journey must spend longer in waters fouled by chemicals and sewage discharge, and may be diverted into leats or trapped behind weirs where they suffer predation, disease and mal-nutrition. One study found fifty percent of smolts never reach the sea. Then, those that survive to return to their native rivers face problems of pollution and siltation and must struggle over indus-trial scale obstructions made more difficult through shifts in temperature and flow caused by climate change.

Phil sighed and raked long fingers through his thick hair. "Migratory fish are under attack from all sides and they are failing."

The objective of this project is to modify or remove as many River Exe weirs as possible. Engaging the support of multiple landowners and contractors, managing technical designs and costs for each weir and actually making it happen; the challenge of the task is not to be underestimated but it could make a sig-nificant difference to these iconic fish.

"If we succeed," Phil said, "we will maximise numbers of spawning fish reaching the redds, increase smolt survival to sea and enhance the ecological health of the river. That's what we're going to do."

Phil's scientific approach, dedication and absolute determination were impressive but it was when I asked him whether he fished himself that his true enthusiasm became clear. His grey-green eyes lit up as he said, "Oh yes, I grew up coarse fishing but now I'm really excited about fishing for wild brown trout in moorland streams."

We spoke the same language. The next hour evaporated as we shared fishing stories, remembering enigmatic dark brownies drawn from peaty moorland pools, winter days brightened by silver grayling and mayfly hatches on warm summer evenings. I told Phil about some of the fish I had caught on this river and Phil told me tales about stalking barbel on the Avon. There in the field he crouched behind a clump of dock leaves, folding his long body to hide behind the small plant, extending his rod arm overhead to demonstrate how he hid from the wily fish, how surreptitiously he cast around the bush and how finally, triumphantly, he secured his barbel.

If the Strategic Exe Weirs project is successful it could improve the straitened fortunes of the noble River Exe salmon. In their long migrations these heroic fish must pass through numerous international waters leaving them vulnerable to over-exploitation, predation, hunger or environmental damage occurring in any one of them. Some areas, such as those in the ocean, may be beyond our control but we can at least offer help to those fish who make it back to the Exe by easing their route from the estuary to their breeding grounds on Exmoor. In this one area where we could exert influence we cannot fail these fish with a neglect that might bring about their final demise. Only the fittest and bravest have made it this far, the heroes of their race, their journey has been difficult and dangerous enough and they are nearly home. Perhaps, at least here, we can offer some real assistance by creating an easier passage through the hammering foam of Pynes Weir and all the others like it on this trembling river.

CHAPTER 32

A Consolation of Grayling

September smoulders into October and the glittering summer songs of swallows and martins are replaced by harsh rasping of fieldfares and redwings raiding the hedges for berries. The trout fishing season sorrowfully ends, next spring and a new season seem far away with winter looming darkly between; but as trout turn their focus from feeding to breeding, grayling come into the peak of condition. This fish has been called The Lady of the Stream due, I suppose, to its polished elegance. One autumn afternoon I set out to try to catch one.

Where a grass field sloped down to a pebbled beach on the left bank of the River Exe, the glassy aisle of the river reflected trees from the far side, sycamore in umber and orange with burnt edges, withies flecked with gold, and tall ash trees a sharp lemon yellow hung with bunches of rusty keys, so the width of the river was lit with colour on water so smooth its movement would have been almost imperceptible but for scattered leaves carried on its sliding surface. Though I have sometimes caught grayling when trout fishing, they can be tricky to find when you want one. They seem not to spread throughout the river like territorial trout but to gather in shoals at a few particular spots.

By tying a dropper like a side-shoot onto my leader I could attach a pair of nymphs, one on each of the two ends – a small

hare's ear with a thin collar of bright orange behind a gold head
and an even smaller pink nymph, no bigger than a lentil. Though
I have often seen grayling rise to take food from the surface, their
undershot jaw is really designed for eating downwards and larger
fish in particular usually feed near the bottom. They are attracted
by bright colours and are especially fond of pink, so I hoped this
offer might tempt one. As I was knotting it all together two sharp
whistles made me look up and smile to see an iridescent blue
flash of kingfisher. A kingfisher is always encouraging.

A little way off the pebble beach, I rolled my pair of nymphs
across the river into deeper water on the far side where they
were pulled along amongst the fallen leaves. With a few casts,
a few steps and a few more casts I fished slowly downstream.
There were rises in the margin but they were tiny, just baby fry.
Here, where the river has slowed with maturity it has softened
in places, bulging with deep, glutinous mud which can be
alarmingly stuggy and in other places stones are slippery with
algae. I moved cautiously.

One cast went well back under overhanging bushes and fell
close to the far bank. Almost at once there was a fish on the
line, putting up a lively performance, glinting silver as he turned
in the dark water. I thought at first it might have been a grayling
but as he came to hand I found it was a brown trout; a very
beautiful one of black-spotted silver, bright as the afternoon
sunshine piercing the ash.

As I walked further along the river a sharp tang of crushed
yarrow rose from my boots' tread, a grey squirrel creaked like an
old gate from tree tops on the far bank and a crow grated a
raucous reply. In the next field I scrambled down the riverbank
and tumbled into the mossy arms of an old ash. When I had
extricated my rod from its twigs and the net on my back from
a bramble, I waded into the river's edge at the foot of a fast
rocky riffle. There should be fish here, I reasoned, as they would
like water freshly oxygenated by the boiling rapids. At least,
trout would like it, so why not grayling.

Grayling are not native to the River Exe but were introduced in the late nineteenth century. A Victorian owner of the Dulverton fish farm, a Mr Langdon, imported grayling ova from the north country, from which he hatched and reared 500 yearlings for a client. At the last moment the order was cancelled and, not knowing what else to do with the fish, Langdon offered them to the River Exe Conservators suggesting he might turn them into the river. This offer was accepted and grayling were released there in about 1896. Yet another story suggests that some ten years earlier grayling were released into the tributary River Lowman from where they quickly spread into the larger river.

Whatever their origins, grayling became well established in the River Exe, though their presence has been subject to controversy; whilst some fishermen were keen to have them to provide autumn and winter fishing, others worried that in competing for food and resources they might overwhelm the population of native trout. This is now believed not to be a problem as brown trout and grayling have differing food preferences, favour different parts of the river and breed at different times of the year, and it seems the two species can live equitably together.

Where white water started to disperse at the foot of the riffle, I cast into slack water on the far side of the river. The line across the fast water had barely tightened when it was seized and taken deep and I pulled a fish through the current as he swung downstream below boughs of elm and sycamore reaching out from the other side. When he came to my net he was another good sized brown trout, richly spotted in red and black and mahogany. Like the first fish, he had taken the beaded nymph which I quickly relieved him of and returned him to the bubbling stream.

It was good to catch fish of any kind and these were particularly splendid trout but my hope was still for a grayling. Pausing for a piece of chocolate, I watched the river as a pair of dippers bobbed and chinked and a wagtail skipped along the pebbly water's edge where fallen leaves were washed up in gold and copper drifts.

A step or two downstream I cast across the river again, rolling my nymphs out under gilded branches and letting the river carry them away. In just three casts I was into another fish. This one was heavy and spun on the line like a propeller, thrashing the water to foam and I held the rod high hoping he wouldn't spin himself off as I drew him across the dragging current. But he didn't come off and pulling the net lanyard from my shoulder I realised that here, at last, was a grayling and as he slid over the rim of the net I saw he was a very handsome fish indeed, as big around as my upper arm and brightly burnished silver. This was a magnificent male grayling in fine condition, his opulent dorsal fin flared green, spotted with black and edged with crimson like an heraldic banner. He had taken the tiny pink nymph and held it in daintily pursed lips below a finely chiselled, aristocratic nose. As I lifted him from the net, his armour of scales felt hard and prickly and when I lowered him into the simmering water he left my hand with a spectacular flourish. A gentleman of the stream.

The Ever Rolling River

CHAPTER 33

Blessings of the River God

I wonder how many times I tried to catch a salmon? Learning to catch trout had not been easy, there are so many skills to accomplish, so many things to remember, and each one of them has to be right every time you cast; but once the basic principles of fish preferences and requirements are understood, finding trout is relatively simple. There are plenty of trout in the river and so there are plenty of opportunities to practise. If you choose the wrong fly or mess up a cast or get in a tangle, well, in the next pool there will be another fish and you can try again. But salmon are another matter. Most of the time they are simply not there.

Then, if a salmon were to be found, and even supposing it could be hooked, landing one might be difficult. Wade relates the worrying story of an actor who fished the Lyn at Watersmeet in the 1860s and hooked a salmon said to have weighed forty pounds. All day long messengers were going to and from Lynmouth relating the latest stages of the struggle while the actor nearly died of exhaustion. At length, 'as the shades of evening were falling the salmon, helped by the wooden bridge and no doubt the devil, left the actor all alone upon the rocks.'

Today there are few opportunities to encounter a salmon at all and those are jealously guarded so it is unsurprising that keen salmon fishermen are generally unwilling to waste the few fish that may be there or the few days when conditions may be perfect to help someone else catch one. I understood that and perhaps in their position I may not have been any more generous but some people were discouraging. "If you want salmon fishing you should go to Scotland," I was told, or "If you really want to catch salmon you should go to Iceland or Russia." "The only way to catch salmon is on a spinner," I was advised (Wade recommended worms) and, most depressingly of all, "If you wanted to catch a salmon here you should have done it twenty years ago." But I wanted to catch an Exmoor salmon this season and I wanted to do it on a fly. I was told that would not be possible.

So, despite the advice of experienced fishermen who knew better, I set out to try. I lost count of how many times I tried. In this vain endeavour I met tremendous generosity from owners of stretches of river where I was made welcome and often given the freedom to fish as much as I liked. But, I learned, the required water conditions were exacting. There should have been a spate of at least two or three days to give salmon a chance to come up from the sea, as they can only do in high water, and then the current should have eased enough to be wadeable and the water must have cleared sufficiently for a fly to be visible. These precise conditions did not occur often so when they did I fished as much as I could, reminding myself, whilst accepting I may have little chance of catching a salmon, if I don't go fishing I have no chance at all.

On the Exe I saw a fish swirling and splashing in a back eddy on the far side of Old Woman's Pool, but it refused every fly I showed it. It could have been a large rainbow trout. I bet it was a salmon. Once at Wonham, and twice at Northmoor, I saw salmon but was unable to attract their attention. One day, on Stoat's Tail, I cast across a run and allowed my fly to wash down into the pool below with no result, so retrieved some line to cast again and as the fly came up close to the surface it was followed by a heaving, roiling bow wave; I couldn't see the fish, it had to be a salmon, but he didn't take the fly and he wouldn't come again. There were days and days of no fish at all. Often I gave up the enterprise as hopeless and took out my little trout rod instead.

Probably the focus here should not be on catching salmon but on why that is so unlikely; the important story is about what has become of them. Numbers of salmon in the River Exe system have fallen so precipitously it would have felt reprehensibly wrong to kill one but, nevertheless, I should have liked to catch one.

It was the 29th of September, the penultimate day of the season. In yesterday's rain I had fallen over slipping on wet grass, hurt my hand and ripped the felt sole off my wading boot. And caught no fish. Luckily I had another pair of wading boots with rubber soles which were less grippy on slippery rock but, on the other hand, safer on wet grass. I had to try again and was acutely aware there were only two more chances. The morning dawned damp and grey with a dearth of swallows and a chill of autumn in the air.

The Exe was the colour of milky coffee and the opaque water did not look fishable; the Barle was a different shade, more like strong tea with a splash of milk and maybe offered some hope. I doubted it, though, when I stopped in Dulverton to gaze sadly over the wall at a river whose bottom was completely invisible. Perhaps it was too coloured, but perhaps it may clear sooner further upstream. The hills were misty and drizzly below a soft grey sky as I drove over the moors, the bracken sodden to a deep red and heather washed to that obscure colour between mauve and tan that has no name – a sort of earthy salmon pink.

At Tarr Steps the water was a little, only a very little better, though the Liscombe stream running into the River Barle just below the Steps was clear. The river must be beginning to fine down, I hoped, and sat in my vehicle drinking a cup of tea from my flask to give it a while longer to do so.

After about ten minutes of impatience I set off upstream. The steep wooded valley held a pool of cold air cupped in its river-rushed hollow which, in soon coming days, would harbour frost. Underwater rocks standing close to the river's surface could just be seen, but the main current ran impenetrably dark.

'The darker the water, the brighter the fly,' I had been advised, so chose a Willie Gunn conehead from my small salmon-fly tin. It was a big, bright fly which I hoped meant it might be spotted in the murky water and the heavy conehead would take it down in the strong current and add an attractive glint of gold.

The first pool I tried was Corner Pool where sandy banks offer easy access opposite a deep run. About a quarter of the river bottom was dimly visible, but only where it was shallowest, and I wondered whether that might be enough and doubted it. After a few casts I walked on briskly, keen to keep moving in the cool valley.

Around a bend the path rises from the river a little and to reach the next pool I walked down over a steepish meadow, through grasses and bracken, feeling glad of my rubber soles. I ducked under hazel boughs brandishing my rod before me like a lance and stepped down to the water's edge beside the riffle at the head of Black Pool. Suddenly, the river seemed to be clearing rapidly and now the bottom was visible almost a third of the way across.

After a few casts at the foot of the riffle I worked my way down the pool, casting towards the opposite bank, letting the fly swing around with the current, just twitching the line in a little as it came across, moving a couple of steps down between each cast. Was that the right thing to do, do you think? I hoped it might be.

About a third of the way down the pool, as the fly drew across the river there was a large swirl behind it. Trying not to get over-excited, I repeated the last cast again. And again. Then it happened, and it felt as though the fly was being shaken by a terrier.

Don't strike, don't strike, I kept telling myself, consciously suppressing the instinct to flick the rod tip up as I would for a trout. The fish moved upstream, I reeled in slack and lifted the rod slowly but firmly, reaching what I hoped was a good tension and tried to maintain it. The fish, of course, had other ideas. He circled the pool, breaking away each time I tried to bring him closer, invisible in the densely coloured water until he reared and bucked at the surface, humping a darkly mottled back.

My largest net was clipped to a ring on the collar of my jacket, it lifted out easily enough and when turned over the hinge clicked satisfactorily into place. But the fish did not want to go in and each time he came close enough to see the net he swirled away again. The rod felt too long, the net handle too short, would the leader break if I pulled too hard, or the hook slip if I allowed any slack? I could not lose this fish.

Eventually the swirls became less energetic and next time the fish came close I pushed the net hard into the resisting current and scooped him in. Yes!

An imposing cock salmon, lightly coloured, sleek bellied and kype jawed, gently stained with the rosy tinge of the river, the same colour as the autumn heather. I unhooked him reverently, supporting him in the current until he was ready to leave when, with a sweep of his broad tail, he swayed back into the disbelieving stream.

I should have liked a hip flask to salute the salmon but was content with dark chocolate and sat on the bank wondering whether that had really happened. The steadily clearing current slid between oak and fern while a robin softly sang a contemplative song of autumn and a pigeon flew upstream, dipping over the water in a long swoop and lifting high into a sycamore to sit in branches whose every leaf was edged in the same rust-red as the river. Fine needles of sunlight lanced the woodland canopy to fall flickering upon the pool like fireflies and far overhead, in the high narrow space between the trees of either bank, a freshening breeze chased small clouds across the brightening blue.

Following a decent interval and a few squares of chocolate I regained my composure and cast again. I had achieved my objective and might have finished there but half the pool lay ahead of me; though I wasn't sure how much the splashing fish would have disturbed it, it was worth another try. After only a few casts the line went dead and somehow I knew it wasn't a rock. If the first fish had felt like a terrier, this one felt like a Rottweiler and as it charged up and down the pool I was aware that this was a fish of considerable substance. With a pumping effort, pulling the rod high then lowering and reeling hard, I brought the heavy fish close enough to see a blurred shape through the coloured water; a long gleaming slab that twisted and contorted, powerfully flexing the rod, pulling the line deep. Each time I brought the salmon close in, it set off again with renewed vigour until, slowing a little, it seemed to have had enough and I slid the net into the water beneath a dazzling silver body. At that it exploded into action once more, disgust plain as it whizzed away – it was not going into that net. And, truly, I thought the fish was right; my twenty six inch net was barely large enough to contain it. Three times it came close and three times set off again, stripping line from the frantic reel.

A drift of fallen leaves had washed up at the water's edge and I contemplated beaching the fish on that, but was anxious not to risk hurting it. Yet I was unable to lift the net onto that furiously thrashing form. In the end I grabbed it by the wrist of its tail, which was thicker than my arm, and hauled the front end bodily into the net.

I wondered at the regal beauty of what I had caught – a neatly mouthed hen fish of finely speckled silver with a fabulous gold cheek and boldly spotted gill cover. For one wild, improbable moment I gazed into her dark, bronze-rimmed eye and she stared back and we saw each other in all our vast differences of form and experience and life, the bright shaft of our eye-contact piercing the gulf of understanding between us; two beings from divergent worlds brought together for a few precious seconds of an autumn morning. She growled as I took out the hook and when I lifted her weighty body and carried her into deeper water my trembling was not entirely due to exertion. As I let her slide back into the current I thought how extraordinary that a fish of this size could disappear so effectively in such a small river, yet the sheltering stream closed over her massive tail as if she had never been there.

All river gods are blessed –
the most blessed of all is the god of the Barle.

CHAPTER 34

The Current of Time

So the rivers run on. Those tweed-clad greenheart-wielding fishermen-writers of the past, Wade, Luttrell, Thornton, Applin and the rest, cannot have seen the water in pools clearer, sunlight sparkling on riffles brighter than it is today. They may not have heard the same sound of motors, that distant tractor or the single engine aircraft humming overhead, yet the symphony of the current cannot have changed much as it follows its course from moor to sea. Those men who will no more walk these riverbanks have, at least, left their words to tell us a little of how it was those long years gone. And we should heed their words, for most of the losses they illustrate so acutely are otherwise unrecorded and might easily be missed.

Memories of past glories effectively highlight the process of change and loss our land has suffered. Losses of some things – cuckoos and nightingales, for example – are obvious to almost everyone but only fishermen notice the loss of fish. Silver forms beneath a silver surface, fluid movements within flowing water, pass unnoticed, unremarked by most people in the human world of air. Many think of fish only in terms of packaged fillets on supermarket shelves where abundance obscures a wild deficit with misleading impressions of plenty. Yet the losses are real and when we understand the scale, the enormity, of what is happening to our land it becomes clear that our hills and valleys, our woodlands and moorlands and especially our rivers need help.

Rivers are not the pristine habitats they appear. Moorland streams may seem to be above the invidious influence of man but each is part of a whole catchment of linked watercourses and, barriers permitting, migratory fish use them all so damage to any part of the system influences the rest. Even though moorland streams escape sewage discharges and run-off from fields and roads with the resultant problems of pollution and siltation, they seem, only marginally less than lowland rivers, to share the widespread deficit of insects and they are profoundly affected by climate change. As water temperatures rise, the southern limit of salmon survival moves steadily northwards. In the same Exmoor streams Wade and Thornton fished, we might expect to catch no more than a tenth of the trout they wrote of catching some hundred and fifty years ago. In just the last twenty five years, wild Atlantic salmon have declined by eighty percent and could disappear from these rivers within our lifetimes (yes, yours and mine).

What is likely to be the future for our upland streams and the rivers they grow into? So many challenges seem overwhelming; it is easy to feel the task hopeless and tempting to admit defeat but how could we answer for that, how could we explain to our grandchildren and how can we convince ourselves it is other people's fault, someone else's responsibility. How can we do nothing whilst idly watching the death of something as eternal as a river?

Many people are doing so much and their steadfast commitment is heartening. Scientists and engineers focus considerable skills and knowledge into the development of solutions for our rivers and streams. They are helped by a stalwart army of supporters; people who generously give money to fund conservation projects or, most precious of all, their time to carry out surveys and undertake practical management work. These are the true heroes – those who care enough to make a real effort, to actually get out there and do something. It is impossible to accept that so much energy and dedication will not be rewarded by some measure of improvement. And there have been gains.

Work monitoring aquatic invertebrates, invasive species and the redds in spawning gravels is building a steadily clearing picture of our river systems. Catch-and-release has now become the norm for rod fishing, since the 1970s there have been significant reductions in the harvest of salmon, international co-operation has reduced over-exploitation in the North Atlantic and netting in the Exe Estuary has ended. Salmon are still declining but the rate of loss has slowed. We cannot consider a possibility of failure but must sustain and build on the current effort, recognise those who work so hard and heed the results of volunteer-driven science, remaining curious and flexible in our response, always nurturing hope.

Every time I visit a river, whether feeling tired and stuffy from work, anxious, sad or stressed, I leave feeling better than when I arrived. Every hatch of dancing river-flies, each swirl or splash of a fish, every dilating rise-ring entices me into the water in hopeful anticipation; then comes the slow change of focus from the business of everyday life to crystallise my attention on river water, bubbles, eddies and current. The fellowship of others I share it with, wagtail, dipper, heron, becoming little sparks of joy as the presence of any of them is revealed. And then the fish – the analysis of where they are lying, what they are taking and how I might try to imitate it in both appearance and presentation requires an intensity of concentration leaving no room for daily concerns. Casting to a rising fish, or to where he might rise if he sees the right fly, is captivating, either through a stubborn persistence when it doesn't work or with enraptured enchantment when it does. Every time my fly is accepted and I flick up my rod, make a little tug with my line hand and *the river tugs back*, like reaching beyond the veil of consciousness and feeling the squeeze of a hand, every fish that comes to my net in all its

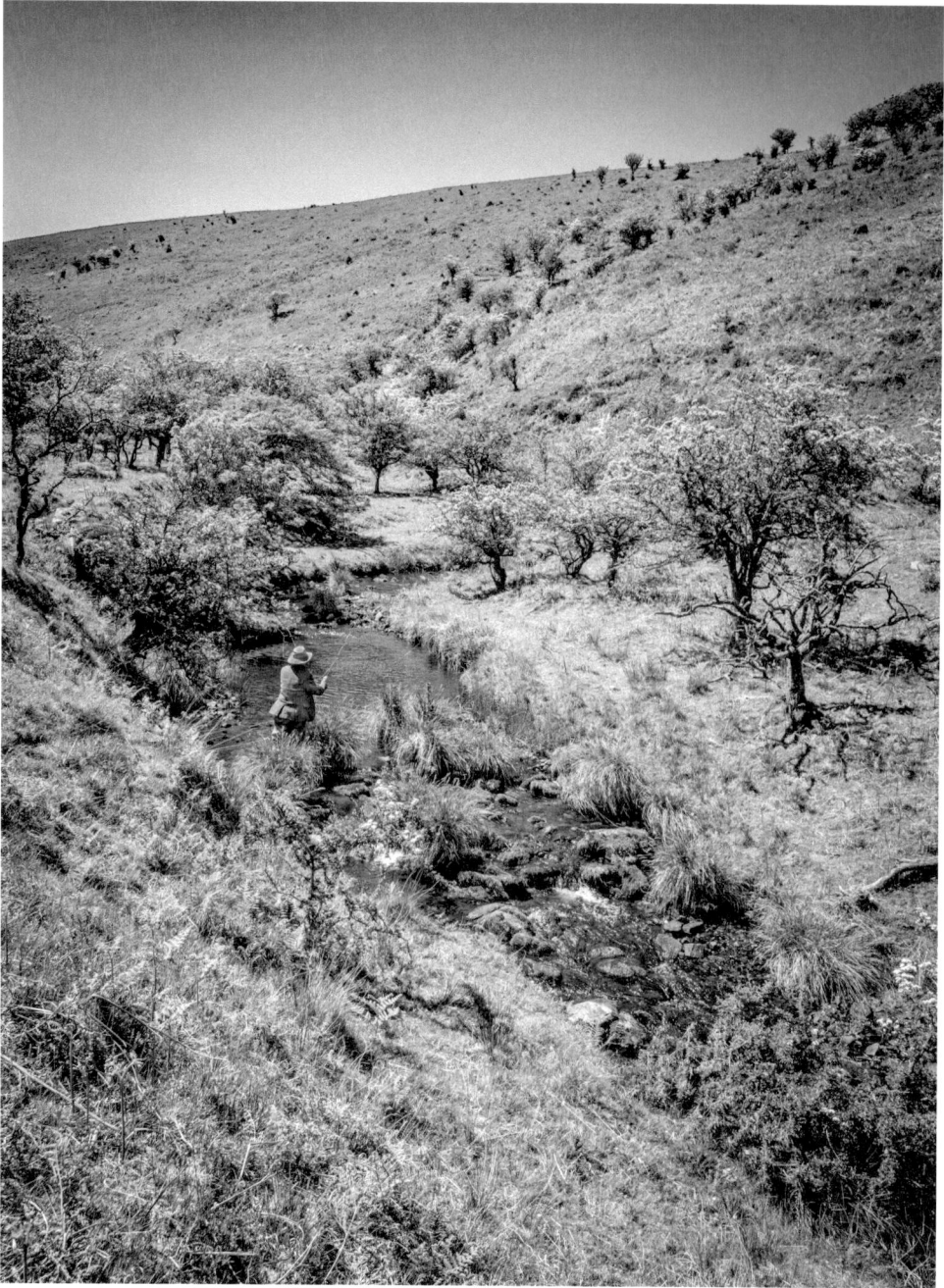

magnificent jewel-studded splendour, every such encounter, every fish, is a gift from the river. The essential quality of gifts is that they are given freely, with no thought of payment, yet their acceptance comes with an obligation, a duty of recognition and expression of gratitude. I have received so many gifts of such incalculable value that a simple thanks is not enough – such generosity demands reciprocation. But what can I give to a river?

My contributions towards river conservation work seem hopelessly inadequate. I try not to be wasteful, not to use toxic chemicals in my home and choose sustainably produced food whenever I can, to tread lightly upon the earth, but I know this isn't enough. Perhaps, though, if I can draw attention to these issues, generate interest and gather more support, perhaps that may help. Could I ever write words sufficiently meaningful to inspire more people to action? Perhaps, if many of us each do a little it may amount to a lot. Could I remind people of what rivers and streams mean to their lives? Might that possibly make a small difference?

What if I wrote about days spent on riverbanks bright with primroses and celandines, in the first flush of spring's warmth. Early memories of walking over dew-wet fields to the river, wellies flumping against thin legs, carrying a jam jar with a string handle to catch bullheads and minnows that wriggled in small childish hands. And later, with a real rod, the little kick on the end of the line, the feel of a wild fish in a wild stream transmitted to yearning fingers: a connection to the vibrant watery spirit of the river. Or summer picnics amongst tall swaying grasses and cool scented water-mint on the riverbank, days brightened by the flash of kingfisher, the grandeur of heron or the thrill of watching a hunting otter pouncing on fish. Of fishing on evenings when the quiet river is looped with interlocking rings of rising trout and, as captivated as a fallen leaf rotating in an eddy, it is impossible to leave until the fly is lost to view in the dimpsey and the river breathes mist over the meadows.

If words could flow like river water what landscapes might they carve, paring away soil and stone to expose the fractured bone of the land, so that people might see and understand. If words ran like rivers what stories might they weave, endlessly braiding past and future as they chatter unheeding past the ephemera of today, telling a longer tale. If words had the reach of rivers, sometimes clear and calm, sometimes raging in fury, how far might they travel and where might they be read. If words moved as freely as water, wandering through a land where parched earth thirsts for stories, what might my words say then, and who might listen?

But the cadence of my words cannot compare with the rhythm of the rivers, the whispers of the streams. My pencil-scratching, notebook-etching words are mere marks on paper and the rivers say it better. Every combe and goyle, every valley of Exmoor is stirred by the voices of waters and the messages they utter are urgent. Do not trouble your thoughts with my words but go instead to the water, listen to the song of the streams, for there you will learn the truth.

THE END

Acknowledgements

A thousand thank yous to so many people who helped make this long-dreamed-of book a reality. Thank you to everyone who invited me to fish their water, lent me their precious books and fishing records, shared their memories or offered help and support in any way. There are many more than there is space for here and those that follow are simply in alphabetical order. Thank you all.

Special mention is due to editors and publishers, Jon and Rose Ward-Allen, for being highly professional, relaxed and easy to work with; to Robin Baker for proofreading and telling me bluntly when my writing was not up to snuff, as well as for his beautiful photography; and, especially, to Claude Wade whose voice reached across the years with advice, encouragement and inspiration and without whom it never would have happened.

Keith Armishaw, River Reads; The Badgworthy Land Company; Ian Baldock, Lillycombe Sporting Club; Tom Barlow; Roger Butcher; John Dawson and members of his fly-tying group; Godfrey Davis; Dulverton Angling Association; Ben Eardley, National Trust; Nicky Green; Mike Groves and the late Molly Groves; Chris Guest; Lewis Hendrie; Oliver Hill; Adrian Howell; Nicholas Kelly, Dunster and Abbotswood Estates; Victoria, The Lady Killearn and Gladys; John Knott, Fly Fisher's Club; Alistair Langford; Fred Leach; Joe Martin; Rupert Martin, Lillycombe Sporting Club; Hugh Maund; Nick Maye, Environment Agency; Ralph and Suzanne Nicholson; Michael Poraj-Wilczynski, National Trust; The Rural Writing Institute; Charles Sands; South West Fishing For Life; Matt Sully, Exmoor National Park; Joshua Thorne, Exe Carnarvon Fishing Club; Tiverton Fly Fishing Association; Philip Turnbull, Westcountry Rivers Trust; Callum Underhill, Environment Agency; Jeremy Whitehorn; Jonathan Woollacott; Tom Yandle; Ueli Zellweger.